THE
NEW CHRISTIAN'S
GUIDE TO
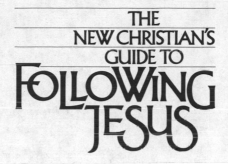

**PROPERTY OF
DARYL GREEN**

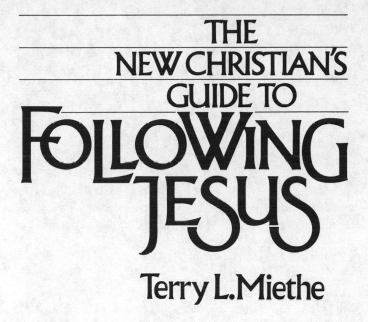

THE
NEW CHRISTIAN'S
GUIDE TO
FOLLOWING JESUS

Terry L. Miethe

BETHANY HOUSE PUBLISHERS
MINNEAPOLIS, MINNESOTA 55438
A Division of Bethany Fellowship, Inc.

Copyright © 1982, 1984
Terry Miethe
All Rights Reserved

Published by Bethany House Publishers
A Division of Bethany Fellowship, Inc.
6820 Auto Club Road, Minneapolis, Minnesota 55438

Printed in the United States of America

Library of Congress Cataloging in Publication Data

Miethe, Terry L., 1948-   .
   The new Christian's guide to following Jesus.

   Bibliography: p.
   Includes index.
   1. Christian life—1960-   . I. Title.
II. Title: Following Jesus.
BV4501.2.M4716   1984   248.4   84-16880
ISBN 0-87123-439-4

Dedication

This book is dedicated with much love to Larry, Paula, Danny, Ron and Kenny: New Christians, babes in Christ and *twice* family!

TERRY L. MIETHE holds the following degrees with honors: A.B., in philosophy and theology; M.A. in philosophy of religion from *Trinity Evangelical Divinity School;* M.Div. from *McCormick Theological Seminary;* Ph.D. in philosophy from *Saint Louis University,* and A.M., Ph.D. in Social Ethics from the University of Southern California. He has been a Babcock Fellow and a Miller Fellow at *USC.*

He has taught at several schools including: Saint Louis University; Fuller Theological Seminary; Regent College, Vancouver, B.C.; and the University of Southern California. He is a member of six honor societies in history, psychology, classical languages including Phi Beta Kappa and Alpha Sigma Nu, the National Jesuit Honor Society. He is presently Professor of Philosophy, Director of the College Honors Program and Director of Liberty Baptist College's Oxford Study Center at Oxford University, England.

Dr. Miethe has over forty articles in print in such journals as: *The Modern Schoolman, Faith & Reason, Journal of the Evangelical Theological Society, Christian Standard, The Disciple, The New Scholasticism, Augustinian Studies,* etc. His published works include: *Thomistic Bibliography,* 1940–1978, with Vernon J. Bourke, *Reflections,* "Atheism: Neitzsche," in *Biblical Errancy: An Analysis of Its Philosophical Roots,* edited by Norman L. Geisler, and *Augustinian Bibliography: 1970–1980; With Essays on the Fundamentals of Augustinian Scholarship.* He is listed in seventeen Who's Whos including: *Who's Who in Religion, Personalities of America, International Who's Who of Intellectuals,* and *Contemporary Authors.* He was a finalist and alternate for a Fubright Fellowship to the United Kingdom.

Preface

Dr. Miethe personally knows the new Christians to whom these chapters originally were addressed, and this gives his words a directness which tends to be lacking when one shoots an arrow into the air and hopes that it will hit a target. But the new Christians whom he knows are like many other new Christians, with the same problems of readjustment to a new faith with its implications for daily life, and his book will be appreciated by a wide circle of readers anxious to know how to make progress in Christian living.

What I especially like about this work is its wise maturity; unlike many writers tackling such an exercise, Dr. Miethe treats his readers as responsible adults and does not talk down to them. The questions for study and discussion and the suggestions for further reading strike me as being very helpful. Dr. Miethe avoids evangelical jargon, but, since some technical terms must be used, he provides a glossary at the end of the work. My supreme commendation of the book would, however, be this: he knows that his readers have minds of their own, and he encourages them to think for themselves. I like the book very much.

F. F. Bruce
Manchester, England

Foreword

I led my neighbor to Jesus. What an experience! It was not at all what I expected. It was easy; I had expected it to be hard. She was more ready to be born again than I was to guide her into that experience. Later on, when she had questions, it was not so easy. Her questions sometimes involved issues that I had never personally questioned. I had lots of searching and digging to do in my new role as "big sister." Many times I found myself researching very basic principles that had been settled in my own heart and mind years before. That experience was good for me in many ways. I found wrong attitudes being exposed that had crept in during my years of serving Jesus. As a child, when I had accepted Jesus, I shrugged off issues that were beyond my understanding, shelving them until I was "older." But when I was "older," I never sought them out again. That is, until someone like my friend asked questions on tough issues like these.

Recently, I was listening to a young man with an undergraduate degree contemplate some decisions concerning his life's direction. He was trying to sort out all the voices he was hearing. Was this job God's will for him, or maybe that graduate program, or even still another direction? It all seemed so complex. There were so many opportunities that it was confusing to me to narrow it all down and help him see the choices that were presenting themselves before him. I finally realized that we were really dealing with an age-old misconception: *God probably wants me to do something that I really don't want to do.* His plans for my future probably won't be much fun for me and probably are, in fact, really awful. It's the "ugly probablys."

I counseled with an overweight lady in my office who thought that God was punishing her with fat because she must have done something really awful. When asked what it was that she had done, she couldn't remember. But it must have been really bad because she was extremely miserable. Another young woman thought that God had made her fat to keep her humble—to keep her from sinning in some awful way that would be inevitable if she had been thin.

A lovely real estate agent with a sharp intellect comes to me. Although she has tremendous ability to meet and cope with the pressures of that demanding career, she cries out to me, "Why is God mad at me today?"

"How do you know that He is?" I asked her.

"Nothing is going right for me today," she said. "Deals that looked solid have fallen through, sellers have taken their property off the market right when I had a good offer." She went on with other complaints that had proven to her that God *must be* dissatisfied with her in some vague way that she couldn't understand. "Otherwise, wouldn't things go right?"

I am sure that you have been faced with some of these same questions and situations in your relationships with people you care about. I expect to have more of this type of opportunity to share the goodness of God and to be of encouragement to those around me. It is because of this expectation that I personally welcome Dr. Miethe's book. He doesn't present pat answers; he provides an opportunity for exploring solutions in a positive atmosphere. It is a "how-to" book of the finest nature. I plan to use it in a home Bible study. I might consider using it to teach a Sunday school class for new believers. I even plan to give it away to "seasoned" Christians that I am sure will enjoy it as much as I have. I will leave one on the night stand of the guest room in my home.

I like this book very much. I am glad that it is here, at last, for people like me and my friends. Thank you, Dr. Miethe. I have looked for a book like this for a long time. Thank you for expressing these issues in such a manner as to leave room for me to think and explore for myself, so I can grow.

Neva Coyle

Contents

Introduction

Another book—oh no! Sometimes I think the greatest thing we could do to help the ecology is stop the constant stream of printing. Stop the senseless waste of paper which comes into our homes daily. "Surely it has been said before, so why another book?" It is true that most of the books printed would never be missed. They waste paper and other resources and pollute the mind of humankind.

Despite the great need to be selective in our use of natural resources, there are at least three justifiable reasons for new books: (1) I have confidence that the human mind has not addressed all the issues, and certainly not in the best ways possible. (2) Every generation must have the age-old issues speak with power to them, in their tongue. (3) The simple truth is that it takes the duplication of books to speak to an audience other books will not reach. I know that this book (however inadequate) will have such an audience.

This is not a question and answer book.[1] It is not a book which lists important questions and then lists short, usually very inadequate, answers. Questions like: How do we know God exists? Why is there so much evil in the world? How can I live the Christian life practically every day? How realiable are the records we have about Jesus? Should Christians today speak in tongues? Why are there so many denominations? Why are my prayers so often unanswered? Can Christian faith help with depression? What is sin? And on and on. I have taught classes, using this format, with hundreds of questions for which people really want the answers. Many such people have been in the church all their lives.

There is a need for question-and-answer books. But all should be aware that such books have limited value. They must not be allowed to think for you. Their often simple answers must be used only as a beginning resource for comparison. They should spur one on to further thinking. In that regard, the same is true of this work.

This book is not a systematic theology.[2] This is not a summarizing of the doctrines of the Christian religion. Further, this work is not systematic in that it is not presented or formulated as a system. Systematic theologies are very important. They are certainly more valuable (in the long run) than question-and-answer books. Yet both have their limitations. A systematic theology, perhaps even more, suffers from being a work written from one point of view. It is usually written to support one particular branch of Christianity.

By all means, examine every systematic theology closely! Even accept their positions if they seem true to you. But also be open to new ways of looking at doctrines and Scriptures. Reserve final judgment always! Remember: one of the marks of a Christian is to obey truth as it is discovered. None of us has a corner on truth! We must constantly be open and willing to examine competing claims, in and out of the faith. This, after all, is central to the claim of Christianity to be Truth issuing from God.

To set ourselves up, no matter how learned, as possessors of all Truth is to make claims to be God! We can know Truth. And all of us have some knowledge of Truth, but none has all. We are fallible human beings who must rely on God's grace and God's wisdom. It would do us all good to remember this. Especially when we look at various opinions about Christianity, including our own.

The purpose of this book is to discuss a series of Christian issues. These are not all the important issues of the Christian faith. Nor are these chapters in any way complete discussions. They are issues of particular importance to new Christians. The hope and prayer is that these new Christians will spend the rest of their lives looking deeply into all aspects of Christianity.

These chapters may be read devotionally, meditated upon, used for further study; i.e., of the Scriptures and books listed, and used as a text for a class on basic Christianity. There are three special sections, besides the footnotes, which will help the reader utilize this book: study/discussion questions at the end of each letter, a glossary of terms, and Scripture reference index. Terms defined in the glossary are set in **bold face type** at their first appearance in the text.

A word is appropriate about how this book came into being. Only in my deepest dreams would the events which preceded its writing have happened! It was over four years since I had returned to my Indiana boyhood home. Several points of pressure helped my family toward Indiana for our 1981 vacation.

Two weeks before we were to leave my sister phoned. Paula had become a Christian! She told us her husband, Danny, was also considering the Christian life, but thought he might want to talk to us. To our surprise, and joy, when we arrived Danny had already accepted Jesus.

Paula was the first member of my family to become a Christian. After she phoned, I had a moment of renewed hope about the rest. "Oh, if I could somehow affect them to accept Christ." This thought had been my constant prayer from the time I came to know Christ.

Events happened, miracles really, and before vacation ended I baptized my brother, his brother-in-law, and my brother-in-law. It had been twenty years since I accepted Jesus as Savior in that same church. My heart burst with the joy you can only know when loved ones come to Christ.

Then on my way back to Los Angeles (somewhere between Indiana and St. Louis), the thought came to me: These babes in Christ had little or no church background. And I would be over two thousand miles away. They needed nurturing. I had reason to believe ministers in the area would help. But I wanted to speak to them as well. Thus, this book came into being.

It was for Larry Miethe, Paula and Danny Dickerson, Ron Yeagley, and Kenny McMullen that the original chapters were written. It is my hope that they, and other new Christians, might find this book valuable. My prayer for all followers of Jesus is that they be constantly on the road to maturity. This little book scarcely marks a beginning. *Study the Scripture, read good Christian lit-*

erature, pray, and ask questions constantly! Indeed, I have much for which to be thankful this day.

—Terry L. Miethe

P.S. It is *still* my constant prayer that the rest of the members of my family will become Christians . . . and others as well.

[1]The following are question-and-answer books: F. F. Bruce, *Answers to Questions*, Michigan: Zondervan, 1973; Frank Colquhoun, editor, *Hard Questions*, Illinois: Inter Varsity Press, 1976; and John W. Montgomery, *How Do We Know There Is A God? And Other Questions Inappropriate In Polite Society*, Minnesota: Bethany Fellowship, 1973.

[2]The following are a few examples of systemic theologies: Charles Finney, *Finney's Systematic Theology*, A new abridged Bicentennial edition, edited by J. H. Fairchild, Minnesota: Bethany Fellowship, 1976; Karl Barth, *Church Dogmatics*, New York: Scribners, 1936-, multi-volumed; Karl Rahner, *Theological Investigations*, Helicon, 1961, 10 + volumes thus far; Helmut Thielicke, *The Evangelical Faith*, Michigan. Eerdmans, 1977 two volumes; and Carl H. F. Henry, *God, Revelation and Authority*, Texas: Word, 1976-, five volumes.

1 / On Being a Christian

This is the first chapter in a series from my pen about the Christian **faith**, discussing some aspect of faith in Christ. My prayer is that each chapter will inform you about and encourage you in living for Jesus.

Now that you are a Christian, all the promises of God are yours to claim![1] Please claim them. This will be a lifelong process which will lead you to maturity, fullness. The Christian life can be incredibly rich. Its richness will, to some extent, depend on your willingness to grow. Believe me, God will bless your sincere desire to know and serve Him. You haven't even begun to imagine what he has in store for you! But remember He respects and honors you. God did not force Himself upon you against your will. And He will not reveal what is in store for you until you are willing and ready. Thus, it is important that you start your life with Him: (a) understanding some of what it is to be a Christian; (b) developing good habits from the beginning; and (c) constantly striving to know more of His love with your mind and heart.

You have accepted Jesus as your savior. Your past sins are forgiven *(I John 1:5-10)*! Count on it. Savior means "one who saves from danger and destruction." In accepting Jesus we are admitting that ultimately our lives were going nowhere without Him *(John 14:1-7)*. You do not have to dwell on your past life. You should not spend hours in sorrow about what you did or didn't do *(Luke 12:22-29)*. You are forgiven. Past and false guilt only hamper the Christian life. What is more, you have the promise of God to forgive your future sins. If you go to Him asking with a sincere heart, He will forgive. Perhaps you have seen the bumper sticker: "Christians aren't perfect, they're just forgiven." How true. You havé just started on the road to the fullness of life.

Now you must make Christ Lord of your life *(Matthew 6:24)*. This is not easy nor does it come quickly like accepting Him as Savior. The dictionary defines a "Lord" as "one having power and authority over others," and "a ruler to whom service and obedience are due." In accepting Him as Savior you have declared your need for Him to help with all of life. You have accepted the God who made you *(John 1:1-5)*, who gave His life for you *(Luke 23, 24)*, and who loves you *(John 3:16)*.

What is it to live under the lordship of Jesus? This is a hard concept to fully appreciate. Indeed, I wonder if any human can completely understand it in this life. But some aspects of "lordship" are clear: We must be willing to live for Him, to turn control of our lives over to One far greater and wiser. We must obey Him as we discover, through the Bible and other means, His will for us. And we must serve Him with our whole lives.

There are some practical implications to this kind of living: (1) We must constantly examine our lives, all the secret rooms of it, to see if we are allowing Christ's influence to grow. You do not become a mature Christian overnight! Anyone who talks as if you do or expects that of you—be very cautious of that person. (2) Every major decision in life should be made with Christ in mind. Ask questions like: Will I feel good about my relationship with God if I do this? Will doing this help my witness for God? How does Jesus fit into this decision? Yes, every decision should be made with Christ in mind! In the end every decision should take second place to our Christian commitment. (3) If we are truly trying to live for Christ, it will be fairly easy to see. More and more our thoughts, time and energy, our personal and financial resources will be used for Him and His Church. As our commitment matures, we will see a continually greater part of who we are in Christ and the Christian community.

I cannot overemphasize the importance of striving to make Him lord of your life. Yet there are some very subtle traps we must avoid. Thomas R. Kelly relates:

"Meister Eckhart wrote: 'There are plenty to follow our Lord halfway, but not the other half. They will give up possessions, friends and honors, but it touches them too closely to disown themselves.' It is just this astonishing life which is willing to follow Him the other half, sincerely to disown itself, this life which intends *complete* obedience, without *any* reservations, that I would propose to you in all humility, in all boldness, in all seriousness. I mean this literally, utterly, completely, and I mean it for you and for me — commit your lives in unreserved obedience to Him . . ."[2]

We must not think that simple doing, even giving up things, means we are living under Christ's lordship. We must be constantly seeking to disown ourselves *(Luke 9:23-25)*! I am reminded of the words to one of my favorite hymns:

"Not I but Christ be honored, loved, exalted. Not I but Christ be seen, be known, be heard. Oh to be saved from myself, dear Lord. Oh to be lost in Thee. Oh that it may be no more I but Christ that lives in me."

When you are new in Christ is the time to develop good **"spiritual"** habits.[3] It is much easier to practice good habits from the beginning. Changing bad patterns developed over years is hard! May I suggest the following for your consideration. Great people of the faith have found these helpful throughout history.
(1) Begin and end every day with prayer. Prayer is basically a conversation with God. Remember: you can talk to God anytime you want!
(2) Read and meditate on a Bible passage daily — usually no more than a paragraph. I suggest in the beginning from the New Testament.
(3) Never miss Church worship unless absolutely necessary!
(4) Set aside a time each day for solitude; i.e., private prayer or meditation.
(5) Try in some way, by example or word, to share your faith in Christ Jesus daily.

I hope this chapter finds you happy and healthy as you begin to live for Him!

STUDY/DISCUSSION QUESTIONS*

1. Why did you respond to God and become a Christian?

2. Discuss some of the promises of God as you understand them.

3. What are the most important parts of being a Christian to you?

4. Discuss the Lordship of Christ.

5. What does it really mean to make "every major decision in life . . . with Christ in mind"?

6. How are you striving to make Jesus Lord of your life?

7. What does it really mean to "disown self"?

8. Which "spiritual" habits do you want to develop?

*You might want to write down your answers to these first questions to review at the end of the book or course.

FOOTNOTES

[1]See: W. T. H. Richards, *God's Great Promises*, Nashville, TN, Abingdon Press, 1973. This is a good beginning devotional with 52 Bible promises (very short) designed to be read one a week.

[2]Thomas R. Kelly, *A Testament of Devotion*. Great Devotional Classics. Arranged and edited by Douglas V. Steere. Nashville, TN: The Upper Room, 1955.

[3]Elton Trueblood has many good things to say about this in: *Alternative to Futility*. You should become familiar with all of Trueblood's writings; e.g., *Company of the Committed*, *The Yoke of Christ*, *Confronting Christ*, *The Life We Prize*, *The Incendiary Fellowship*, and *The Best of Elton Trueblood: An Anthology*.

2 / What Is Faith?

What constitutes faith in the Christian sense is a very important question. The concept of faith is perhaps the most basic doctrine of Christianity because this idea is at its very heart. All other Christian doctrines can be understood and integrated only in the light of its meaning. If faith is the most basic of all Christian doctrines, it is also the most misunderstood. Many people believe it is something **mystical**. Some believe it to be a gift of God.[1] Others believe to have faith is to go against reason or knowledge. H. L. Mencken once said, "Faith may be defined briefly as an illogical belief in the occurrence of the improbable." None of these are true!

I have often said that the greatest victory of Satan would be in allowing us to have a religious vocabulary; e.g., words like faith, **stewardship, justification, baptism**, etc., but not understand what the language really means. Satan wouldn't care if we did go to church regularly as long as we don't understand the distinctly Christian words used there. This is exactly the situation with the average Christian. Therefore, I charge you from the very beginning to find out what the words mean! Be aware that asking questions may not be enough. Many older Christians do not know the answers themselves. Learning the meanings may take study, **diligent** research. And "faith" is one of the first words you should learn about.[2]

"Faith" appears only two times in the Old Testament (*Deuteronomy 32:20* and *Habakkuk 2:4*). The word is found 307 times in the New Testament. The New Testament was originally written in Greek. When you consult a Greek dictionary for definitions of "faith" *(pistis)* two essentials are found at the heart of Biblical teaching: (1) trust or acceptance: belief that Jesus is Lord, with acknowledgement of His resurrection; and

(2) intellectual content: the revealed truth that is firmly believed, and is reflected in the life of the believer.

Paul Little said in his book *Know Why You Believe*, "It is not enough to know *what* we believe. It is essential to know *why* we believe it. Believing something doesn't make it true. A thing is true or not regardless of whether anyone believes it." In *Your Mind Matters*, John Stott explains faith as "a reasoning trust, a trust which reckons thoughtfully and confidently upon the trustworthiness of God." Faith, according to Josh McDowell's *Evidence That Demands a Verdict*, is "the assurance of the heart in the adequacy of the evidence." This seems to reflect the significance of Hebrews 11:1. Yes, we *must* know why we believe in any age, especially today.

We do not find "blind faith" anywhere in the New Testament. Even the "trust" or "acceptance" part of faith is not blind. God has provided us with more than enough evidence we can test. We have historically reliable evidence that can be tested in the same way any history can. Thank God for it! Dr. D. Martyn Lloyd-Jones makes a very important statement in commenting on Matthew 6:30:

> Faith, according to our Lord's teaching in this paragraph, is primarily thinking; and the whole trouble with a man of little faith is that he does not think. He allows circumstances to bludgeon him . . . . We must spend more time in studying our Lord's lessons in observation and deduction. The Bible is full of logic, and we must never think of faith as something purely mystical. We do not just sit down in an armchair and expect marvelous things to happen to us. That is not Christian faith. Christian faith is essentially thinking . . . . Faith, if you like, can be defined like this: It is a man insisting upon thinking when everything seems determined to bludgeon and knock him down in an intellectual sense. The trouble with the person of little faith is that, instead of controlling his own thought, his thought is being controlled by something else . . . . That is the essence of worry . . . . That is not thought; that is the absence of thought, a failure to think.

You need to begin reading in the field called **"Christian Evidences"** or **"Apologetics."**[3]

It does not matter how *much* faith we have. What matters is the object in which we have our faith. John Warwick Montgomery, *The Shape of the Past*, says: "If our 'Christ of faith' deviates at all from the Biblical 'Jesus of history', then to the extent of that deviation we lose the genuine Christ of faith." Saving faith literally means to "believe into." It denotes a faith which takes a person out of themselves and puts them into Christ. This kind of faith carries an intellectual assent that ties itself with the strongest possible bonds to Jesus. It is trusting a person — Jesus, the Christ.

The two aspects of faith mentioned earlier make it not a passing thing, but a continuing attitude of life. Christian faith is not a way of life, it is life! If we are not living as Christians we are only existing. In the Greek *pistis* ("Faith") we have the first turning in "trust" and "acceptance." In *gnosis* ("knowledge") we have that continual growth to which faith advances. Faith begins with that initial trusting aspect and little knowledge. But faith must become more and more informed as we mature with knowledge. It can be said that faith is a conscious mental desire to do the will of the God of the Bible.

In the words of Isaiah 41:21, God issues a great challenge to false gods: " 'Present your case,' the Lord says. 'Bring forward your strong arguments,' the King of Jacob says" *(New American Standard Bible)*. Clark Pinnock, in *Set Forth Your Case*, writes:

> Certainly the Lord himself does not shrink from the demand for authenticating credentials on the part of the gospel. Our good news is an accredited claim and bona fide offer. Our confidence in its objective truth is reflected in our zeal for its defense and proclamation.

If God does not shrink from the demand for proof, why should we?

What is faith really? Probably the best answer can be found in I Peter 3:15, "But set apart Christ as Lord in your hearts,[4] always being ready to make a defense to everyone who asks you to give an account for the hope that is in you, yet with gentleness and reverence." The word "faith" nowhere appears in this Scripture, yet both aspects of its meaning are clearly seen. All Christians stand beneath this command; but many do not respond to it.

Jesus said: "If you love me you will keep my commandments" *(John 14:15 — compare also John 21:15-17)*. The Apostles called people to the intelligent faith in Jesus because

He was and *is* God! All of us who claim the name of Christ should do the same because *we* are also commanded to be ready at all times. This obviously demands a life of dedication and disciplined study. The biblical concept of faith seems to presuppose (or assume) the ability of every Christian to defend his/her faith. Take note of Acts 17:2,17 where the text says that Paul "argued" the rationality of the Christian faith (see also *I Peter 3:15; 2 Peter 1:16-21;* and *Acts 9:26-31*).

Thus, there are several aspects involved in Christian faith: (1) Accepting Jesus as the resurrected Son of God based on evidence. (2) The act of reflecting God's Truth revealed in the Bible in how we live our lives. (3) Knowing not only what we believe, but why we believe it. (4) As we mature, faith is being able to call people to an intelligent commitment to Christ by giving reasons for our belief.

I hope you are willing to pay the price to grow in Christ. It is a high price, but well worth it!

STUDY/DISCUSSION QUESTIONS

1. List five or ten words that are part of Chrisitian vocabulary. What do they really mean? Do any of them relate to each other?

2. What two concepts are "at the heart of Biblical teaching" regarding faith?

3. Discuss the idea of "saving faith." How does it relate to your life?

4. How is a person's faith affected as he matures in Christ?

5. Discuss the reason(s) that knowing *why* you believe is as important as knowing *what*?

6. What does it mean to be able to "defend" your faith? Why is it important?

FOOTNOTES

[1]Some groups of Christians believe Scripture teaches that faith is the special gift of God given only to those whom God has chosen. Ephesians 2:8 reads: "By grace you have been saved through faith, and *that* not of yourselves, *it* is a gift of God." But in the Greek text of that passage there is only one pronoun, not two; and it does not agree grammatically with the word faith. (The pronoun is neuter in gender, while "faith" is feminine.) According to all grammatical rules, the gift cannot be faith! What is referred to here is God's gracious gift of salvation which none can merit.

I realize this is a rather technical point of Bible study. But it points out two things you should be aware of: (1) the Bible is a book with great depth; (2) there is much for you to learn!

[2]See my booklet: *The Christian's Need To Know* and read everything you can find on faith and reason or the reasonableness of faith, etc.

[3]Besides the books already mentioned in this letter, see: Richard L. Purtill's *Reason to Believe*, Eerdmans, 1974, and Clark Pinnock's *Reason Enough: A Case for the Christian Faith*, Inter Varsity Press, 1980.

[4]The word "heart" in the Bible often refers to the mind, the center of a person's being. It is a person's thinking ability which most truly marks him as created in God's image *(Genesis 1:26-27)*.

3 / Living the Christian Life

What is living the Christian life? How do *I* go about living it? This is a question which Christians *should* be asking constantly. I see people everyday who have spent their lives in the church but don't seem to know the answer. They have sat under good preaching, some of them, yet they don't know! I am amazed! Why is it that preaching so often doesn't seem to have much effect? As a preacher (sometimes) I have a theory about this. Of course, I am assuming good biblical preaching and you very often cannot. Also, preaching should be varied in content and level of delivery so as to speak to the different levels of the listeners. First, many people do not really listen. Second, listening is not enough. Church members should ponder what is said. It would help if all preachers provided paper for notes, preached with a **systematic** outline, and constantly encouraged their members to think on the sermons. Third, preaching, even at its best, is not enough. Time should be provided for discussion of the sermon if real understanding and growth are to occur.

Fourth, and most important, people do not understand living the Christian life from hearing a sermon because preaching is the product of the study and effort of the preacher. There is a great old saying in education which rings true: "Tell me and I will forget, show me and I might remember, involve me and I will understand."[1] Yes, it takes great effort on the part of each individual Christian to be able to answer the question. As we said in Chapter 2, *each* Christian must know not only what he/she believes, but why. Every Christian must make the content of the Christian faith his/her own. Just sitting under good preaching is not enough. In and of itself, even great preaching will not mature you. *You* must study, pray and ponder!

Many Christians are really asking: What is God's will for my life?[2] What does God really want *me* to do? They are wanting God to reveal a detailed blueprint for life. God doesn't work that way. That would not only be too easy, but it would go against our **free will**. It would take the responsibility out of our hands and make us robots. God does have a general and specific will for our lives. His general will is that every human being be saved; i.e., accept Jesus as Lord and Savior and live for God. His specific will depends upon *your* talents and abilities. You are expected to use what He has given you in the best way you can to serve Him. Some people have the idea that if they are not suffering, they are not really serving Him. This is not true. In fact, using our talents and abilities will be joyous. So your life, personality, skills must be ordered for Him.

I must tell you a personal story about living the Christian life. It actually happened the summer after I really understood what it meant to make a commitment to Christ. I was working in a factory during the day and helping my father plow each evening. Of course, you realize working on a production line doesn't often take a great deal of mental concentration. Therefore, I would sing hymns silently in my mind as I worked. Every minute my thoughts were God-related. I was constantly thinking about living for Him. It was as if my need to live for Him had been burned into the front of my mind! When I came into contact with another person, my immediate thought was: How can I affect that individual for God? I trained myself to always think that way.

After singing all day silently at the factory and out loud on the tractor, and thinking about sharing God's love with everyone I met, at night I would bathe and go outside our house to spend about a half hour in prayer before bed. During this summer I was also praying for and witnessing to my family. My mother came to believe that I had turned into a religious fanatic. Where I grew up, it was all right (at least tolerated) to be any kind of fanatic other than a religious one. My parents supposedly knew a man who, after becoming a religious nut, turned into an actual nut (mentally). Being convinced it was just a matter of time until I followed that fellow to the funny farm, mother called (of all people) a Christian minister in town. She wanted him to talk to me and set me straight before it was too late. I had never met the man. He agreed to talk to me. We made an appointment.

I was never so disappointed in my entire life. I told him of my commitment, thoughts, desire to live every minute for God. To which the minister replied: "Now young man when you grow older you will mellow and . . . ." I was living the Christian life, but a little too seriously. This error happens all too often. New Christians are excited and actively seeking to live for God. Then they run into many in the church who show them a different example. Before long the new believers are saying to themselves: "Maybe I had better conform. After all, they have been Christians much longer than I. Maybe apathy, laziness, and spiritual ignorance is the way. Maybe I shouldn't be so happy in my faith. Maybe I shouldn't be so quick to share it with others."

The point of the story is this. Living the Christian life *is* a constant mental desire. You should be joyous in it. You should be thinking about it. You should want to share it. Don't let anyone tell you it is only when the fire is out that you are a "real" Christian. Keep the fire alive always! Think, rejoice, pray constantly (I Thessalonians 5:15-18).

Here are some rather practical aspects of living the Christian life: (1) Become more Christ-like. Study the life of Jesus, his interaction with people, attitude, and try to apply this to your life. Pour over the Gospels for every hint of how He lived, then model it. He was our example in all things. Again we see the need for disciplined study. Which brings me to the next point. (2) The more we mature in Christ, the more we will know how to live the Christian life. You simply cannot become a mature Christian by accident. The real reason most Christians do not know how to live the life is they have only a minimal understanding of their faith. They try to live their entire lives on the first grade level. They never engage in disciplined study to find out of what the Christian life really consists. This lack of understanding breeds misunderstanding, and, worse, apathy.

If preaching, as discussed earlier, is inadequate alone, so are Sunday School classes. You cannot sit in a class in which no one (except *maybe* the teacher) has prepared beforehand, in which everyone takes a turn reading, and in which a list of questions are quickly discussed, and expect to mature in

Christ! You must personally discipline your life in study, prayer, **worship**, and **fellowship** to grow. No one can do it for you. There are no shortcuts. It takes much time and effort. So quite simply, the more you learn about your faith, the more you will be able to apply it to living.

(3) Try always to live the Golden Rule: "Do to others as you would have them do to you." Treat everyone the way you would want to be treated. Almost everyone recognizes this as the most basic principle of conduct. Yet few realize it comes directly from the Bible *(Matthew 7:12* and *Luke 6:31)*. Oh, how much better our lives, and the lives of others, would be if we only burned this rule into our conduct.

(4) There are two related truths once their importance is really understood that will help you live the Christian life: First, we are always in the presence of God. "We are always in His sight. He sees our every action, indeed our very thought."[3] He knows your heart. You cannot deceive Him. If we realize that God is always with us, right beside us, closer than any friend, there will be things we simply would not want to do. It will not always be a matter of right and wrong, but of appropriateness. Certain things will simply not be appropriate with God. Second, because God is constantly with us, we can always talk to Him. We so take this for granted! We can talk to Him every minute of the day. We can ask Him for help with any problem. We can seek strength in any situation. In short, He is our constant companion. Why not take advantage of this help in living the Christian life?

I will close this chapter with a quote from C. S. Lewis: ". . . the Christian idea of 'putting on Christ,' or first 'dressing up' as a son of God in order that you may finally become a real son. What I want to make clear is that this is not one among many jobs a Christian has to do; and it is not a sort of special exercise for the top class. It is the whole of Christianity. Christianity offers nothing else at all."[4]

STUDY/DISCUSSION QUESTIONS

1. Why is "good preaching" *not* enough to help you mature in Christ? How can you make good preaching a more effective tool in your life?

2. What talents do you have that you are or could be using for Christ and the church?

3. What talents do *you* want to develop for Christ?

4. Discuss the "Golden Rule." Give some examples of how you practice it.

5. "We are always in the presence of God." What does that mean to you?

6. What does C. S. Lewis mean when he says that "putting on Christ . . . is the whole of Christianity"?

FOOTNOTES

[1] This slogan is one used by the Oregon College of Education at Monmouth, Oregon; a school founded in the 1850's as a frontier college by two of the sons of Alexander Campbell, it later became a state school, one of three in Oregon's teacher training system.

[2] See Paul Little's, *Affirming the will of God,* a little booklet from Inter Varsity Press. Little has some other good books as well.

[3] D. Martyn Lloyd-Jones, *Studies in the Sermon on the Mount.* Vol. Two, Eerdmans, 1960, p. 9-20.

[4] C. S. Lewis, *Mere Christianity,* Macmillan Company, 1943; p. 166. You should familiarize yourself with all of Lewis' works. He was one of the greatest Christian writers of the twentieth century.

4 / Day by Day

This is the fourth chapter from my pen about the Christian faith. Number three was entitled, "Living the Christian Life." I listed four hints to living the life. This study is an extension of that one. The process of living the life of faith is one that we must try to progress in daily. The ultimate quest of this life is to know, love, and follow God more fully "day by day!"

Thomas Aquinas, one of the greatest Christian thinkers, spoke of the "eternal now."[1] Truly speaking the past and the future never really exist. The past exists only in our memory; the future only in our hopes and desires. It is always now. It is this now in which we must be concerned about living for God.

The past should engage us only as the lessons learned enable us to live now for God. Again guilt need not be a part of the Christian life. The future should be our concern only in that we set goals to mature and serve our God. Anxiety over our lives is not necessary for the Christian. The fact that it is always now can be a great comfort to us. We need—indeed we must—not be overly concerned about past or future. All we need to do is concentrate on living for Christ now, this very moment. *I* am becoming convinced that the more we realize this the fuller life in Christ will be! This is a lesson I am just learning.

The modern musical, *Godspell*, includes a song that has become generally popular:

> Day by day, dear Lord,
> Three things I pray:
> To *see* thee more clearly
> To *love* thee more dearly
> To *follow* thee more nearly . . .

Few people realize that the words of this song have a very old origin. This formula has been a common chant or prayer for hundreds of years.

In 1534 Ignatius of Loyola founded the Society of Jesus, the Jesuit order. In his *Spiritual Exercises* he wrote of a similar desire (No. 104, the end of No. 109, and toward the beginning of No. 130). A prayer of Richard of Chichester, who died in 1255, ends with the words, "O most merciful Friend, Brother and Redeemer; may I know thee more clearly, love thee more dearly, and follow thee more nearly."

Our time seems enamored with the notion that any statement or idea more than one hundred years old is not worthy of consideration, unless, of course, it is contained in a book considered an antique by collectors willing to pay a handsome sum for it. And then the real value is not in the thought or idea, not really in the object, but in the money for which it can be sold. Beware of the materialism and the throw-away mentality of our time!

Here in the words of this old prayer I find a beautiful, heartfelt expression of what it has always been and always will be to live the Christian life.

TO SEE THEE MORE CLEARLY:

Historically, the ability to see has been associated with knowledge and the mind. Indeed, in Saint Richard's prayer of the thirteenth century the word "know" stands where "see" does in the modern song. This involves the believer's knowledge of God. God clearly revealed Himself to us in the person of Jesus, and "to see more clearly" proposes a greater knowledge of Christ.

The word "clear" refers to something sharply defined, to be made intelligible. The Christian's life must be an attempt to know Jesus better with each passing day—to know both with comprehending and intimate knowledge the living Word. New Testament Christians learn about Him in his written Word, the Bible. Thus, to "see" or "know" Him more clearly means we must be dedicated to Bible study throughout our lives.

TO LOVE THEE MORE DEARLY:

Paul tells us it is through knowledge and discernment that a Christian's love becomes plentiful or wealthy in its fullness

(Philippians 1:9-11).[2] The basis of this knowledge is the fact that God extended both **revelation** and **salvation** to us. Our response to God is a vertical and horizontal love relationship: God has given us **grace**, and we respond with faith, that is, acceptance based on evidence.

To love the Lord we must first know Him. Once we know Him we will want to love Him "more dearly." This kind of love naturally flows to others. The Christian then becomes the means of extending the love of God to others as an ambassador of God in the ministry of **reconciliation** *(2 Corinthians 5:17-20).* To know God is to love Him and to love Him is to share that love with others!

TO FOLLOW THEE MORE NEARLY:

The word **"disciple"** is based on the verb "to learn." It denotes a pupil, a learner and, especially with regard to the followers of Jesus, an adherent to Him. A disciple of Christ must, by definition, be a learner and a doer. Obviously, the "doing" must be based on the "learning." How can we be "doers" if we have not first learned to "know" God and, through study of Scripture, His will for our lives?

"Disciple" implies a personal relationship which shapes the whole life of the one discipled. Like no other teacher, Christ embodied His teaching. The Christian is a disciple only when he or she adheres to Christ in both thought and action.

So today, dear Lord, for all of us who earnestly desire to live the Christian life, three things I pray: to *see* you more clearly, to *love* you more dearly, to *follow* you more nearly day by day, day by day . . . day . . . by . . . day!

STUDY/DISCUSSION QUESTIONS

1. What are the implications of being concerned about living for Christ now?

2. Why is the "materialism and the throw-away mentality of our time" so dangerous for the Christian?

3. How can we "see" Christ more clearly?

4. Discuss what "loving God more dearly" means to you.

5. Discuss the implications of being a "disciple of Christ.'

6. How does a Christian "discern" God's will for their lives? (See footnote two.)

FOOTNOTES

[1]See Vernon J. Bourke's *The Pocket Aquinas*. New York: Hafner, 1953. Also for a biography of Aquinas: Bourke's *Aquinas' Search for Wisdom*, Milwaukee: Bruce, 1965, is considered a classic.

[2]Discernment or "depth of insight" means intellectual understanding. In Paul's day this word had an established meaning relating to the perception of good and evil in particular instances. Intellectual understanding is necessary for the Christian's ethical choices. God's will in particular instances is finally "a matter for the Christian himself to discern and decide, a matter of insight into the given situation." For Paul this is not some vague moral instinct. Paul does not divorce "insight" from "knowledge." They always go hand-in-hand. And both are nurtured by living in the community of believers; i.e., the Church.

5 / God's Love for Us

This article will try to shed some light on the most profound truth of Christianity: "God loves us!" Immediately, if like me, you will ask: "How can this be?" "How can God love such an insignificant creature?" I must confess, in addressing this subject, to feeling just like A. W. Tozer when he said:

> Yet if we would know God and for other's sake tell what we know, we must try to speak of His love. All Christians have tried, but none has ever done it very well. I can no more do justice to that awesome and wonder-filled theme than a child can grasp a star. Still, by reaching toward the star the child may call attention to it and even indicate the direction one must look to see it. So, as I stretch my heart toward the high, shining love of God, someone who has not before known about it may be encouraged to look up and have hope.[1]

I am like the child of whom Dr. Tozer spoke. Only in my very best moments, and then far too infrequently, have I caught small glimpses of the radiant glory of God's love. Even less often have I been a beacon of that love to others. My hope is that we will see and radiate His perfect love more as we mature in Him!

GOD'S LOVE:

Any discussion of this awesome subject must start with the following realizations: (1) God is love (I John 4:8,16). Now this is not the same as saying that "love is God." "The words 'God is love' mean that love is an essential attribute of God." Love is part of God's very being, but it does not exhaust His **inherent** characteristics. We can learn about God's love from some of His other qualities. God is self-existent. He was not caused to be. From this we see that God's love had no beginning, nor can it have an end.[2] God is infinite; thus His love is without limit. God is holy, so His love must be pure in an absolute sense. Because God is God His love reveals an "incomprehensibly vast, bottomless, shoreless sea before which we kneel in joyful silence. . . ."[3]

(2) "We love, because He first loved us" (I John 4:19; also 4:10). We must realize that the human ability to love exists only because we are created in God's image! God is a personal being. He, as any person, "thinks, feels, and purposes and carries these purposes into action, (and) has active relationships with others."[4] It is because God is a person that we have personality. It is a person's thinking ability which most truly marks them as created in God's image. If the ability to think is one of God's greatest gifts, a second just as important is the ability to love! The very best of what it is to be human, the ability to think and to love, is a reflection of God in us. Of course, this, too, can be tarnished by our selfishness.

Perhaps one of the most tragic and lovely stories of God's love is found in Hosea, the Old Testament **prophet**. A prophet's life was never easy.

But surely the hardest lot fell to Hosea, for this prophetic calling involved him in nothing less than a broken marriage. Yet as he lavished His love on a worthless woman, and felt the bitterness of her desertion and adultery, and as his love still pursued her and took her back after it all, the whole episode was the most potent symbol of the love of God, free and undeserved, yet spurned and suffering, and still pursuing His truant people with a faithfulness that knows no defeat, to restore them at last to the privileges of the covenant which they themselves had broken.[5]

This is true love. This is our story, for we also rejected God's free and undeserved love for a time. But thanks be to God, we do so no longer!

(3) God loved us so much that He gave us His Son. The Bible is found in miniature in these, the most beuatiful of all words: "For God so loved the world, that He gave His only begotten Son, that whoever believes in Him should not perish,

but have eternal life" *(John 3:16, also I John 4:9-10)*. Here we see **selfless** love! We did not, indeed could not, merit it. Yet God loved us so! It is only in this act of God that "love" has meaning, substance, and value. It is here (and at the foot of the cross) that we witness the very standard of love.

JESUS' LOVE:

We see the Father's love reflected in selfless gifts. The Son's love is revealed for us in the giving of self. (1) He "emptied Himself, taking the form of a **bond-servant**, and being made in the likeness of men" *(Philippians 2:5-7)*. How difficult that must have been. How much love that must have taken! He was equal with God. The Scripture says, "He existed in the form of God." This was true humility. He was willing to come and live among us. He came not as a king or a member of the rich ruling class, but as a humble servant. He was born into the household of a poor carpenter. Truly this boggles the mind, and yet there is more to the love story.

(2) He was willing to live among us, to live as we lived. He was tempted in all things even as we, yet He did not falter *(Hebrews 2:18 and 4:15)*. He is our example in all things.[6] He suffered the treatment of humans; i.e., rejection, mockery, even beatings, etc. He knows our plight. He can understand and help because He lived it too! And yet there is more . . .

(3) He not only lived for us (a level of existence so far removed from His very nature), but He willingly died that we might live. Paul tells us in Romans 5:8, "But God demonstrated His own love toward us, in that while we were yet sinners, Christ died for us." "God initiates His love for us without our ever doing one thing to merit His favor or concern. (In fact, it is quite clear that if we went on the merit system, we would merit His wrath.)"[7] Yes, the Cross of Jesus is the ultimate manifestation of God's love. It is not just an empty symbol, but the way to life eternal for us *(Romans 6:1-11)*.

He did not just die, but rose to new life. "The cross without the resurrection would be the ultimate *example*, but the cross with the **resurrection** becomes the *dynamic* making possible for us the way of the cross." With the resurrection of Jesus we are confronted with the living Christ. He is a transformed presence able to bring us through death to life.[8] Christ died for us, for our sins. But the New Testament says even more about the love of God: He rose that we might live in God's presence eternally! Again, in Jesus' example, we see the very meaning of love.

GOD'S LOVE IN US:

No discussion of God's love for us would be complete without some words about how we relate to that love. We are instruments of sharing God's love with individuals. Many need it so desperately in a world of such pain. The real task, the *only task* of a Christian is to share God's love! The word most often used in the Greek New Testament to signify God's love for humankind is *agape*. This is also the word used for the love which should bind people to one another, especially Christians in the Church.

Its classic description is found in I Corinthians 13:4-8a, and 13:

> Love is patient, love is kind, and is not jealous; love does not brag and is not arrogant, does not act unbecomingly; it does not seek its own, is not provoked, does not take into account a wrong suffered, does not rejoice in unrighteousness, but rejoices with the truth; bears all things, believes all things, hopes all things, endures all things. Love never fails; . . . But now abide faith, hope, love, these three; but the greatest of these is love.

I always use this Scripture in my wedding ceremonies. It is a challenge, for the couple becoming one, to perfect love.[9] Ultimately they can only become one in Christ. The best single definition of *agape* is: intentionally, intelligently willing the best for another no matter what the cost *(See Galatians 5:14-15)*.

There are many ways God's love must show itself in us: (1) First, we see it showing itself as good will. "Love wills the good for all and never wills harm or evil to any."[10] This must be an attitude of life we continually develop within. (2) When we think kind thoughts, but more, do kind deeds, God's love is showing. (3) As we meet the heartfelt needs of others with sacrificial giving, God's love is present. (4) God's love is most truly a reality when we willingly, happily share of who and what we are (our very life's essence) with another. This is what God has done for us. This is our glorious privilege in Him!

"The love of God is one of the great realities of the universe, a pillar upon which the hope of the world rests. But it is

a personal, intimate thing, too. God does not love popula-
tions, He loves people. He loves not masses, but men. He
loves us all with a mighty love that has no beginning and can
have no end."[11] Be happy and share God's love!

STUDY/DISCUSSION QUESTIONS

1. Why is it so important to share "God's love for us"?

2. What does "God is love" mean?

3. How does your ability to love relate to God (I John 4:10,19)?

4. How is God's great love for us shown most dramatically (John 3:16)?

5. Discuss what Scripture means when it says that Jesus, "emptied Himself, taking the form of a bond-servant . . ." (Philippians 2:5-7).

6. How does Jesus' death on the cross relate to your being forgiven of
your sins?

7. Why is the bodily resurrection of Jesus so important to Christianity?

8. How do you reflect God's love to others?

FOOTNOTES

[1]A. W. Tozer. *The Knowledge of the Holy.* The Attributes of God: Their
Meaning in the Christian Life. New York: Harper & Row, 1961, p.
105

[2]C. S. Lewis once said the only place that a person was totally, really free
from the love of God was in hell.

[3]Tozer, *Ibid.*

[4]R. T. France, *The Living God.* A personal look at what the Bible says
about God. London: Inter Varsity Press, 1970, p. 19.

[5]*Ibid.,* p. 85-86.

[6]See John R. W Stott's *Basic Christianity.* London: Inter Varsity Press,
1958, especially chapter three.

[7]Peter E. Gillquist, *Love is Now* Grand Rapids, MI: Zondervan Publishing House, 1970, p. 55.

[8]Frank Stagg, *New Testament Theology* Nashville, TN: Broadman Press,
1962, p. 123.

[9]Gillquist, *Ibid* , chapter six.

[10]Tozer, *Ibid.*

[11]*Ibid.,* p. 109.

6 / The Humanity of Christ

I hope this discussion finds you reaching out to share your love and your faith! The last section tried to shed some light on God's love for us, the most profound truth of Christianity. The humanity of Christ is related to God's love. I alluded to this in Chapter 5. Perhaps no miracle of Christ equals that of His sinless life! Christ's humanity is very important to an understanding of our faith and nature.

Some words are appropriate about God's humanity. A God who shares existence, communicates with, and gives the free gift of grace is really related to us! He has a relationship with us in **covenant**. I realize talking about God's humanity may sound strange, but is it? I believe our very knowledge of His deity points to His humanity. "It is precisely God's deity which, rightly understood, includes his humanity."[1]

Many people misunderstand what it is to be human. How often have you heard, when someone does something wrong, or disappoints another: "After all, they are only human." Used this way, the state of being "human" is inseparably tied to something base, sinful, or in error. The whole idea comes from a certain interpretation of the fall of mankind into sin with the very beginning of our race. We do not have time here for a theological discussion of the "**original sin**" or Adam and Eve, etc. But it is important to realize that we are not *more* human because of our sin, but *less*. We were created as human beings and in God's image. Our rebellion away from God made us less human, not more.

God is **absolute**. He is also really related to us. We may not be able to understand this completely, but that does not make it less true. In history many philosophers have made the mistake of not realizing this truth. They have destroyed the delicate balance between the two. God is made either totally separate from us, our world, and our knowledge (wholly other, **transcendent** in an extreme sense) or just a projection of the mind or the collective consciousness of humankind (only **immanent**). God must be at one and the same time both the supreme example of transcendent absolute *and* really related to us. Karl Barth said it well:

> In this divinely free volition and election, in this sovereign decision (the ancients said, in His decree), God is *human*. His free affirmation of man, His free concern for him, His free substitution for him — this is God's humanity. We recognize it exactly at the point where we also recognize His deity. Is it not true that in Jesus Christ, as He is attested in the Holy Scripture, genuine deity includes in itself genuine humanity? . . . In the mirror of this humanity of Jesus Christ the humanity of God enclosed in His deity reveals itself.[2]

It is because we are so related to God that we can know, love, and share Him with each other!

It is in the person of Jesus Christ that we see both true God and true man. (In theology this is called His "dual nature.") He was both fully God and fully man at the same time.[3] Jesus was and is the **Mediator** and **Reconciler** between God and Man[4] Thus He reveals them, God *and* man, to each other. In Jesus' becoming fully human, we see God's desire not only to be compassionate Savior, but also our friend and partner.

This, after all, is the beautiful truth of the story of the Good **Samaritan** *(Luke 10:30-7).* The Samaritan not only took pity on the one who was robbed and beaten, but he cared for him personally. He gave his resources to see to his recovery. The compassion we see here, so unexpected and so undeserved, must speak to us of what God has done for us. Just as the Samaritan freely cares for one who is not of his own, so God freely cares for us who are not His by virtue of our sin. God is *truly* humane! In His very deity He is human.

Some moderns have come to the point that the "complete humanity of the historical personality of Jesus of Nazareth" is a very "great embarrassment for faith."[5] But our faith must preserve and protect both His deity and His real humanity. He ate, drank, slept, got tired, was sorrowful, rejoiced even as we. He even need to pray! As I said in Chapter 5, He was tempted in all points as we.

The true humanity of Jesus is very important to our faith in at least four ways: (1) Christ's humanity guarantees a truly real **incarnation**. If He was not man in every point, then He did not really come down to our level. He would have left some part of our burden untouched. But Jesus did come all the way. He did stoop to a unity with mankind. The Son of God really became flesh and lived with us *(John 1:14)*! The word "flesh" is a very potent word, perhaps the strongest in Scripture referring to man's lowliness. It suggests the completeness of His humanity. It is used of a condition as far removed from divine glory as is possible. Paul, the Apostle, even says that Jesus was in the "likeness of sinful flesh" *(Romans 8:3)*. Certainly Paul witnessed powerfully to the deity of Jesus. He also witness to the true humanity of Christ.

There is another element of the incarnation which is very important to us. God did not force Himself upon us! He did not come as sovereign King demanding our worship. Rather, He came as humble servant asking us to make our own decision. Only because the deity of Christ appears in His humanity can we really choose to live for Him, in His example.

(2) The humanity of Christ provides a necessary foundation for the sacrificial death of Jesus (known as the **atonement**). Jesus could only stand in our stead before God because he *was* human. We often take for granted the significance of His death for us. He did not just die, but lived for us. He had so much compassion that he cried, wept for us! Thus, Jesus' manhood is the very cornerstone of our being restored to harmony with God.

(3) Christ's humanity secures the reality of a perfect example. He felt the burden He carried for us so greatly that even He prayed to God about it *(Luke 22:39-44)*. In our times of temptation it is everything to realize that He also was tempted! In Jesus, the Christ (the Word made flesh), perfect righteousness is put within the sphere of our existence. "The fruits of the Spirit are but the aspects of Jesus' character."

46

(4) Christ's humanity indicates the direction of our destiny after death. Because He rose to new life, we too can believe in the life to come *(Romans 6:9-12)*. Because He was triumphant we will transcend this mortal existence. If He was our example, He was also our "test case." If He was not fully human we could not expect our humanity to last!

Yes, in Jesus of Nazareth we see that divinity and humanity are *not* mutually exclusive, not hopelessly separated! They were not so in Him, and because of our relationship toHim, they are not so for us. We exist because of God. Originally our nature (our humanity) was created by Him. Christ restores our true humanity! We have the glorious privilege to know and love Him. We also have the serious responsibility to share God's humanity, Christ's humanity, and our humanity with each other. May your life be increasingly *human*!

STUDY/DISCUSSION QUESTIONS

1. How is God really related to us?
2. What sense does it make to say that "God's deity . . . includes His humanity"?
3. Discuss what it is to be human.
4. What does the story of the Good Samaritan *(Luke 10:30-37)* tell us about God's love?
5. Discuss how Christ's humanity related to His deity.
6. In what ways was Jesus' humanity important to our faith?
7. How do we share both deity *and* humanity with others?

FOOTNOTES

[1]Karl Barth, *The Humanity of God.* Richmond, Virginia: John Knox Press, 1960, p. 46.

[2]*Ibid.*, p. 51.

[3]There are various views as to how this mixture was a reality: It is well known that a certain difference exists between the Reformed (Calvinistic) doctrine and the Lutheran doctrine. They both accept the Creed of Chalcedon: the two natures were not mingled, but they are united in one person. The Lutherans teach the *communicatio idiomatum*; i.e., the blending of the two natures in an historic person, Jesus.

[4]See Emil Brunner's *The Mediator: A Study of the Central Doctrine of the Christian Faith.* Philadelphia, PA: Westminster Press, 1962. This is a formidable theological treatise.

[5]*Ibid.*, p. 328.

7 / The Importance of Bible Study

It would be impossible to overstate the importance of serious Bible study for the Christian. Study of Scripture is indispensable for people who claim allegiance to Christ. In spite of this importance, *many* Christians never really engage in serious study. Leander Keck says:

> The Bible is more revered than read because most people do not know how to read it with understanding; hence they don't read it at all. Consequently, it is the most neglected resource of our time. Even people who hail it as "the precious Word of God" often fail to catch its inner dynamic. True, reading the Bible can be a formidable undertaking; but it can also bring one into the presence of God. It can do this if we are willing to read it seriously.[1]

For the Christian the Bible is the most valuable book in the world. This is because, to believers, Scripture is the record of God revealing Himself to each of us. What more important reason could there be for really studying it? The Bible is not a record of our attempts to find God, but of God's divine self-disclosure to us. Henry H. Halley says it rather well in his classic *Bible Handbook:*

> Apart from any theory of inspiration; or any theory of how the Bible books came to their present form; or how much the text may have suffered in transmission at the hands of editors and copyists; apart from the question of how much is to be interpreted literally and how much figuratively, or what is historical and what may be poetical; if we will assume that the Bible is just what it appears to be, and study its books to know their contents, we will find

48

there a Unity of Thought indicating that One Mind inspired
the writing and compilation of the whole series of books;
that it bears on its face the stamp of its Author; that it is in
a unique and distinctive sense THE WORD OF GOD.[2]
I believe the evidence[3] overwhelmingly supports the reliability of
Scripture.[4]

The word "bible" comes from the Greek "biblos," which
simply means a book. Several other titles are used to refer to the
Bible; e.g., "the Scriptures" or "the Writings" (I Corinthians),
"the word of God" (Hebrews 4:12), "the Written Word," etc.
For our purposes the Bible consists of sixty-six books, 39 in the
Old Testament (a covenant or agreement) and 27 in the New.
Although we cannot go into them here, there are several divisions within the Old and New Testaments; e.g., books of law,
history, poetry, prophecy; the Gospels, one book of history
(Acts), epistles, one book of prophecy (Revelation).[5] Within
these wider divisions there are many others.

The Bible is not just God's self-disclosure. It is also the
means by which sinful people may know God's plan of salvation. We may know that God forgives our sins and gives us
eternal life through His Son, Jesus. "For the Son of man
came to seek and save the lost" (Luke 19:10). "You shall
know the truth, and the truth shall make you free" (John 8:32).

I should say something about what the Bible is not. It is not
a book about death. It is a book about life, true life here and
hereafter! Perhaps this is the reason we often use the Bible for
comfort in the presence of death. It is also not a textbook of
science, history, psychology or even ethics. It is not a textbook
at all. When its message touches these subjects we have every
right to expect it to be accurate. But we must also be very careful not to read things into it, say, in the realm of science, which
are not really there. Frankly, it does not often speak in some of
these areas because this is not its purpose.

Our need for food to nourish the physical body has been
compared to our need to study the Bible for our spiritual well-
being. In fact it has been said that if we starved our physical
body like most of us starve our spiritual one, we would not be
alive very long. This is exactly the problem with the "faith" of
most church members. Food, exercise, and rest are essential
for the health of the body. Some have likened exercise to
Christian service, rest (or renewal of energies) to prayer, and

food to the Scripture. These are very good **analogies**. Certainly people who love God, and want to be used by Him, *must* study His Word.

R. C. Sproul lists two myths, reasons why people say they do not study the Bible[6]: (1) The Bible is too difficult to understand. "You have to be a theologian to make sense of it." The truth is, most theologians become theologians because their initial study of the Bible and commitment to Christ drove them to want to reach the highest possible level of proficiency. They did not become theologians so they could read and study the Bible. Rather, they became theologians by spending years reading and studying God's word. Sproul says:

> When we express this myth, we do so with astonishing ease . . . . If we can read the newspaper, we can read the Bible. In fact, I would venture to guess that more difficult words and concepts are expressed on the front pages of the newspaper than on most pages of the Bible.

The more we read about what we find in the newspaper, the more we will understand of what it speaks. The same is true of the Bible. In fact, life is a constant learning process. If we stop learning, we die; in more ways than one: at home, on the job, in life, etc.

(2) The Bible is boring. Biblical characters are presented in the text of Scripture as full of life. "Their lives reveal drama, pathos, lust, crime, devotion and every conceivable aspect of human existence." Maybe we are reading the wrong parts of Scripture, at least to start. Many start reading (and give up) in the genealogy lists of Genesis.[7] Maybe we are reading an outdated version that we cannot understand. And maybe we are just mouthing a convenient excuse for not being disciplined enough to read at all, let alone study in depth. After all, most of us have resources (like a minister, Christian bookstore, friend) who can direct us to understandable versions of the Bible, good Christian literature, and Bible studies. Study suggests labor, serious, diligent work.

There are many reasons to study Scripture:

(1) As we said early in this letter, the Bible is the record of God revealing Himself and His love to us. We study the Scripture to find out about God.

(2) The Bible is a source for faith in the beginning. Later it helps us maintain our faith. "So faith comes by hearing,

and hearing by the word of Christ" *(Romans 10:17)*.

(3)   The Bible is where we find out God's plan of salvation. It tells us how to attain a life that is lived in a right relationship with God *(Ephesians 6:17)*.

(4)   Study of the Bible helps us to not only mature in our knowledge of Christ, but to live the Christian life *(Psalm 119:11,105)*. It provides guidance for the Christian which helps us make ethical decisions in relation to everyday events.

(5)   An understanding of Scripture helps us to be sensitive to other's needs. It gives us perspective on serving others, injustice, war, love, etc.

(6)   And very important: study of the Bible helps make our lives a witness and example in interpersonal relations and community service.

Something must be said about the attitude with which we study the Scripture. I have known many people who study the Bible to use it in the support of personal prejudices (don't confuse me with the evidence; my mind is already made up!), racism, and every other evil attitude and action. To be sure, most of us are guilty, at times, of using the Bible to support our preconceived attitudes and opinions. But most of us are not so evil as to use the Bible straight out, openly to support our racism, *etc.*

What I am really concerned about here is a much more subtle evil. I have known one particular individual for over 16 years who reads the Bible, studies it, takes pride in being rather knowledgeable about it, prays at every meal (with the TV blaring), has been a leader and officer in the church. Rarely in life have I found anyone so filled with hate, self-satisfied, selfish, opinionated. unchristian in their attitude of life. The best and worst word. the most appropriate, to describe that individual is "bigot;" i.e., intolerantly devoted to their own opinion.[8]

After a lifetime in the church, studying a Sunday school lesson regularly, there is no indication of even an elementary understanding of the Christian life. But there is a great deal of evidence to support the fact that the Bible *is used*, selectively to support pet opinions, etc. Woe to that person *(Philippians 3:17-19)*!

We must be very, very careful about how and why we study the Bible *and* what we do with it. We must not go to the

Bible to find out what we think it says or should say. Rather we must go to it with an open heart and mind to learn what it would say to us! We should study it with a sense of awe and expectancy, a desire to be transformed, made new. We must be *teachable* (willing to learn)!

The purpose of Bible study must be to make Christ real to us. The more we meditate upon God's word, the more we should become Christlike! We must not be unkind, **intolerant,** judgmental in our attitudes! Even if we are "sure" that ours is the one true, correct view, the attitude with which we express that view may tell others as much about our Christianity as what we believe!

You have embarked on a life of learning, the Christian life. But learning that will not be a drudgery, boring, without any real purpose. This learning is the very key that will unlock the door to understanding your new commitment to Christ and to a new *and* joyous life!

STUDY/DISCUSSION QUESTIONS

1. Why study the Bible?
2. Discuss why the Bible is "not a textbook of science, history, psychology, or even ethics."
3. Why do people consistently misuse the Bible? How can you avoid this?
4. What is the purpose of Bible study?
5. Discuss several different versions of the Bible available to you. Which do you like best, and why?

FOOTNOTES

[1]Leander E. Keck, *Taking the Bible Seriously* New York: Abingdon Press, 1962, p. 7.

[2]Henry H. Halley, *Halley's Bible Handbook: An Abbreviated Bible Commentary.* Grand Rapids. MI: Zondervan Publishing House, 1965, p. 22.

[3]We could not even begin a competent discussion of the evidence here, but the following books will get you on the road: John R W. Stott, *Understanding the Bible*, Glendale, CA: Regal Books of Gospel Light Publications, 1972; Norman Geisler, *A General Introduction to the Bible*, Chicago: Moody Press. 1968; F. F. Bruce, *The Books and the Parchments.* The Languages, Canons, Manuscripts, Versions, History and "Lost Books" of the Bible, Westwood, N.J.: Fleming H. Revell Co., 1963, and also by Bruce, *The New Testament Documents: Are They Reliable?* Grand Rapids, MI: Wm. B. Eerdmans Publishing Co., 1953.

[4]There is a great debate over the reliability of Scripture today which takes many sides. Many are in danger of excluding other believers too quickly and too harshly because they differ in rather minor points of interpretation. Even if we disagree strongly with another over the nature of, say, errors in Scripture, we should not be quick to separate ourselves or drive a wedge between them and us. Many times a kind and open attitude will reveal that there are points of agreement more numerous and just as important as the admittedly important disagreement(s). We will certainly all benefit by starting our continuing discussions, even if they were initiated on a point of disagreement, by assessing areas of agreement and then progressing in our sharing. After all, who of us can really be so sure of the absolute truth of our knowledge that we can afford to cut off dialogue?

For one side of the debate see: Norman Geisler (ed.), *Biblical Errancy: An Analysis of Its Philosophical Roots*, Zondervan, 1981. This is a discussion of the effect of various philosophers on our views of Scripture. I have chapter six on Nietzsche in the volume.

[5]*Ibid.*, Geisler, *A General Introduction to the Bible*.

[6]R. C. Sproul, *Knowing Scripture*. Downers Grove, IL: Inter Varsity Press, 1977, p. 13-31.

[7]There are many ways to study the Bible: by book, topical studies, biographical studies, great Bible passages, paragraphs, chapters, etc.

[8]The word "bigot" comes from the middle French word for hypocrite, play-actors. It refers to one who has made up their mind before looking at the evidence (or little or none), and who gives an outward appearance of being one thing when inside they are really another.

8 / When I'm Good Enough

The bulk of this article was originally written to my father. Some years before it was written, he had been involved in an accident that at the time we thought threatened his life. While he was in the hospital I resolved to talk to him about becoming a Christian. Based on his reply, I felt then that he had a basic misunderstanding of faith and the church.

We are just coming out of a very anti-institutional and anti-organized religion phase in American culture. You can still feel the effects of it. I share this with you now because I believe many have a misunderstanding of the purpose of the church. In the next portion I will say more about the importance of church membership.

Since my father's accident the idea that you had to be "good enough" to become a Christian gnawed away at me. I was lying in bed at 3:30 in the morning unable to sleep, thinking about my father. Thoughts I had been having repeatedly for years began to crystallize in my mind. That very day I had worked from morning until dark finishing a lengthy article on the Christian's responsibility in regard to education.[1] In the evening my wife and I had discussed how hard it is to remember your thoughts if you do not write them down when they come to you. I arose a little before 4:00 a.m. to write this down so I would not forget.

My father is a *good* man! For years he has struggled to raise his four children to become "good" adults. Many men in his little Midwestern community who know him would give the "shirt off their backs" to help Dad. They know how he has given help to many others. He is regarded well by others, as a good man.

My father is an astute armchair theologian. Dad probably

received some of his knowledge in this area from childhood training. Grandmother Miethe was immersed in an old horse tank. On at least two separate occasions in my young life as a dedicated Christian, Dad's penetrating and simple advice was both surprising and of great spiritual help. I remember them well. I had dedicated my life to the **ministry**, not really understanding what that meant then.[2] Having transferred to Bible college that past year, I was at home for the summer. Doubts about God's will for my life began to arise. Late one evening when I asked Dad about the problem, he said, "If the Lord had not wanted you in the ministry, He would not have led you this far." Rather simple advice, but it comforted me, especially coming from him.

On another occasion when I was really upset over the actions of some Christians my father said, "I thought when you were **immersed** you were supposed to have been **born again**." I replied that I *was* supposed to have been reborn. He said, "Then why don't *you* act like it?" The idea was clear and straightforward. Don't let those other people bother you so much. Just be sure *you* act like the Christian you are supposed to be.

But my father is not a Christian. I am rather sure he believes in God and in Jesus as the Son of God. Yet he does not live for Him. Once when he was in the hospital, hurt badly by a tractor overturning on him, I asked why he was not a Christian. Dad replied that he knew to be a Christian meant to serve God totally. There was no halfway. And he was not good enough yet to do that. But when he became "good enough" he would become a Christian. That was some eight years ago[3] and to my knowledge he is still not serving Christ.

This is written in the hope that my dad, and the many like him in every community, will realize that our accepting Christ as Savior and serving Him as Lord is not contingent upon "when I'm good enough."[4]

What Is Moral Perfection?

A new understanding of moral perfection is prerequisite. The kind of "perfection" my father is waiting for is not possible in this life. To be complete in all respects, flawless as it were, is not possible for men in their own strength. The word "perfect" in English usage expresses a state or action completed at the time of speaking. To be perfect would require that all people be gods. Most have no trouble agreeing that this is not the state of man.

A better understanding of the way to moral perfection is necessary. We can be perfect, complete and lacking in nothing, only in Christ *(Romans 8:3)*. Jesus was the only one who lived to perfection. In the Sermon on the Mount, He admonished His hearers, "Therefore you are *to be* perfect, as your heavenly Father *is* perfect *(Matthew 5:48)*. Jesus has just given them the Beatitudes, the "original draught of essential Christianity" *(Matthew 5:13-16)*. This is a sketch of the character of those already in the kingdom and a "description of the quality of the ethical life which is now expected of them." In Matthew 13-16 we see this Christian reacting to and being reacted to by the world. The last section of this chapter *(5:17-48)* deals with the relationship of the Christian to God's law.[5] In Matthew 6 we have a picture of the Christian living his life in this world, in God's presence, and in active submission to Him.

It is obvious from these two chapters that this sermon demands a quality of ethical conduct which is lofty to be sure. It is also obvious that "it is neither an impractical ideal nor a fully attainable possibility." This kind of perfection is possible only as we strive constantly in Christ, with the indwelling help of the Holy Spirit, to attain that which is *fully* attainable only when God will be "all in all." Reaching perfection, then, is a lifelong process possible only with God's help.

Human Nature and Perfection

A clearer understanding of even the best of human nature is necessary. Even the apostles were not perfect. What Christian would not like to have only a fraction of the influence on the world that some of these had? And yet Peter denied his lord three times before Christ's death *(Matthew 26:69-75)*. Paul, who turned the world upside down for Jesus in his lifetime, seems to have had trouble doing what he *knew* he should: "For the good that I wish, I do not do; but I practice the very evil that I do not wish" *(Romans 7:19)*. Paul goes on to say that it is only through Christ that a person can be made good enough. I realize there has always been disagreement over whether this passage is talking about a man who is already a Christian or one who is not. But the distinction is not important here for all *must* agree, if one is to take the Scripture seriously, that Christ is needed to help us live for God. Later Paul begs Christians to be like him *(Galatians 4:12)*. If the apostles needed Jesus' help to live for Him, and can still be a pattern for our lives, surely all of us need Him, too.

The Christian Message and Perfection

A more basic understanding of the Christian Message is essential. Jesus did not say that He would accept us only after we had, or thought we had, become good enough. If Jesus did not lay down any such condition, do we have that right? The whole message of Christianity is that "He loved us first" *(I John 4:12-18)* "while we were yet sinners" *(Romans 5:8)*. Surely if God exhibited a love for us so strong and beautiful that He was willing to send His son to die for us just as we are, the least we can do is to accept His proffered love and the help that goes with it. The great beauty of the Christian message is *precisely* this point. We do not have to love God in secret, nor do we have to be "good enough" to accept Him as Lord and Savior. We don't have to merit His love even if we could! He gives His love and help in moral perfection to anyone who desires it. Can't we all use such help?

A more studied understanding of the purpose of the church is needed. Assuredly those people who condemn the church because the people in it are not perfect misunderstand the purpose of it. The church exists for sinners, men and women less than perfect. I will not argue here that everyone in the church lives as he should or even that he makes a good effort to do so. We have plenty of Christians who obviously do not. But again this misses the point.

One must not reject Christianity on the basis that some or all of the people they know who profess to follow it do not. One rejects it because it is not true, and, therefore, cannot work for him or for us. The point is that Christ died for *you* . You have the glorious opportunity of accepting His help, to *help* and to *be helped* by other Christians. Many Christians *are* striving to live for Him. They can help us and we can help others. Indeed, the church *is* a place for sinners. It is a place for the weak and strong, a place where God's help is available.

Perfection, A Stumbling Block

A deeper insight into the rationale behind this idea is required. Eventually, if we are going to be honest, we need to re-examine our reasoning. Maybe what seems on the surface to be a noble desire; i.e., being good enough, turns out in reality to be an old excuse! Are we really putting off accepting Christ as Lord and Savior because we love Him and want to be perfect in acceptance? Or are we failing to accept Him because we are afraid of the change that might come about with His help. Peter Gillquist in this book, *Love is Now*, says:

> The end result of God's love flowing unconditionally from Him to us is that a love response is activated within our lives. His love becomes creative; it molds us into new persons. God's love does not *demand* a change; it *produces* one.[6]

If moral perfection cannot be achieved on our own, if Christ can help us to be so, if even the apostles needed His help, if the heart of the Christian message is that He accepts us as we are, if the church is for sinners, if we are not just making an excuse, and *if* we really believe He is God (if this is the problem, then we need seriously to study the evidence behind the claims of Christianity; i.e., the fields of Christian evidences and apologetics), and love Him, we will no longer say, "when I'm good enough. . . ."

My constant prayer is still that my father, and all the good men like him, will give Christ a chance to accept them as they are now!

STUDY/DISCUSSION QUESTIONS

1. Discuss the causes of the "anti-institutional" and "anti-organized" religion phase in American culture.

2. Discuss the difference between being merely a "good person" and living for Jesus.

3. What is "moral perfection"?

4. What is the purpose of the Church?

5. Do you have to be "good enough" to accept Christ?

6. How can people who have the erroneous idea that perfection is necessary to become a Christian, whether they really believe it or are using it as an excuse, be helped?

FOOTNOTES

[1] See my booklet: *The Christian's Need To Know.*

[2] I did not have any preconceived idea that this necessarily meant the ordained clergy, serving a church. And now I realize it does not mean that—every Christian is a minister, but more on this in a later epistle.

[3] It has been an additional six years since this was written.

[4] I realize you have already become a Christian. Yet I believe this letter may help you have a better understanding of faith and the church. At the very least it should help you witness to those who use this excuse to avoid facing Christ! It also speaks to the opposite form of the excuse: "I am a good man. I don't need Christianity."

[5] See: D. Martyn Lloyd-Jones' excellent two-volume work, *Studies in the Sermon on Mount*, Eerdmans Publishing Co., 1960.

[6] Peter Gillquist, *Love Is Now*. Zondervan Press, 1971, p. 70.

9 / The Importance of Church Membership

We live in a very peculiar age in *many* ways! I doubt if I will get much disagreement on that statement. In Chapter 8, I mentioned we are just coming out of a very anti-church (really anti-institutional) stage. We are also coming out, hopefully, of an extremely selfish era. Many have named the Seventies the "me decade."

Because of the combination of these factors many people who claim to be Christians, young *and* older, are asking: "Why should I be a church member?" This shows one of the peculiarities of our age. I really doubt if any but a very few would have even thought of such a question in generations past. After all, a Christian was a living part of the church!

I have heard every imaginable excuse for not being a part of a church. Once, as a young minister, I was making a hospital call on one of my church members. When the man in the next bed heard who I was he said, with obvious pride, "I can worship God just as well on my tractor out in my field. I don't have to go to church. After all the church is full of **hypocrites**." His statement raises several thoughts. What is "worship"? We will treat this subject in depth in future chapters. Worship is an attitude of life. It is not just "going to church" or the doing of any overt act. It must be a lifelong process which enhances the quality of one's existence.

Truly you can worship God on a tractor out in the field. This was my first reply. Then I asked: "Do you?" In other words, what is your attitude of life? Surely a part of this must be a very frequent, conscious (intentional) desire to communicate with God, praise Him, serve Him, *and* to share His love with others. This is all part of worship. So you see, while God can be worshipped in the field on a tractor, you must also worship Him elsewhere. Some aspects of worship involve, even demand, other surroundings and, yes, even other people.

Second, you will get no argument from me about hypocrites. The church does have more than its share. But then the church exists for sinners.[1] If everyone were perfect, I doubt if we would need churches. There is much truth in the statement: If you find a perfect church, don't join it for then it will no longer be perfect. The perfect church would be the one without people.

Another thought which must be expressed—perhaps there are positive reasons to go to church. If you are a Christian, if you are not a hypocrite, and if you understand what it means to say "Christ died for all humankind," then you have an obligation to make the world in which you live, and the church, better. More on this a little later in this section.

You are a new Christian. I want to strongly encourage you to immerse yourself in a specific church. The church of your choice. But let me be very honest with you. There are churches which I could not join. Some would not have me! Some I should not join. I could not honestly join a church that has "tests for fellowship" or "**creedal** statements" to which one must prescribe other than, "I accept Jesus as the Christ, the Son of the living God, as my Lord and Savior." I could not join a church which will not allow membership to a person on the grounds of race or color, or that even taught a subtle racism.

I would always try to find a church that respected the Bible as the word of God and accepted the historic truths of Christianity; e.g., the **pre-existence of Christ, virgin birth**, the sinless life of Jesus, the death on the cross, the bodily resurrection, the **second coming**, etc. I would want a church that believed every Christian is a minister and which expects its members to function as such according to their talents and abilities. I would want to be a member of a church which tried to live according to New Testament teaching and precedent.

I should say a word about the phrase: "church of your choice." There are good and bad reasons for choosing some churches and rejecting others. To some extent the "correctness" of these reasons will depend on individual factors. I think generally it is a good idea to join the church nearest your home that tries to be a Biblical church according to your best understanding of what that means. The personality of the minister(s) is not a good reason to accept or reject a church.

I am not at all convinced that very large churches are the way to go.[2] One good reason, to me, for going to a church some distance from home rather than a larger one close by "may" be that the smaller church needs you more. It is more mature to choose a church on the basis of what you can do for it, than what it can do for you. But every church differs, and circumstances are not the same. I am of the opinion that some, perhaps even many churches, should close their doors. I believe some churches witness stronger in a negative way than in a positive one. Alas, the choice is yours. Once made, you should give that church everything you have to make it the very best church it can become! You should probably leave it only if you find it is adversely affecting your Christian life, your family, or you move away, etc.

It might be helpful to say something about what constitutes the church. The Church is the living body of Christ on earth. It is not a building, or a denominational name, or a charismatic personality! Thus, when you become a Christian, you become a member of the Church, the body of Christ. Any local congregation, a church, is in some measure a part of the Church. It is this to the degree that the individual Christians in it are maturing followers of Jesus. The trick is to try to find a church which is as much a part of the Church as it can be,[3] or to make one as much a part of the Church as you can. In the New Testament that fellowship of persons in Christ is variously described as the *ekklesia* (church), the body of Christ, the *koinonia* (fellowship) of the Spirit, the flock, the elect, royal priesthood, holy nation, God's own people, etc.[4] In the simplest sense it is a group of believers who are striving together to live, share, and grow in a life committed to God, the Father; Jesus, the Son; and the Holy Spirit!

There are many crucial reasons for being a member of a local church:

(1) *The sustenance of Christian fellowship.* Yes, we who claim to be Christians *need* the church. We

have a great need for Christian fellowship! It can help us grow, give us people with which to share our sorrows and joys, and help make us richer humans! Our own spiritual faith, our lives, need Christian fellowship. John Wesley once said that there was no such thing as a solitary Christian. Our faith is not only a witness to the world, but also must be lived in love and shared with fellow believers. I cannot imagine people claiming to be Christians who do not realize this great need. The early Christians found that personal faith led to a corporate church life *(Acts 2:46)*. Our own attitude may tell us more about how we will get along in a church than anything else!

(2) *The church is the family of God.* Can you imagine being part of God's family but never taking part in the life of the family? I cannot! I suppose this may be another way of stating reason one, but with a slightly different emphasis. Being a part of a real family has to be one of the greatest joys in the world. It does not just happen. It takes work and commitment to make any family, more than an hour or two a week. Being part of a loving family is a joy not just because of our needs, but because it enriches all who care enough to work to make it. This is a very important reason to become a member of a church. It shows everyone where you stand. You want to be a vital part of the family with family responsibilities.

(3) *The church is a Christian college.* It is, or can be, a place of great learning, where we learn from each other, where we can have a check and balance on our personal opinions and attitudes. God obviously intended that His people should be taught *(Ephesians 4:11-12)*. The church must be a family of scholars gathering to inspire and teach each other God's way. Just like any good school, part of a church's function is to provide the corporate discipline which helps us personally.

(4) *The opportunities for service.* No one has denied that you are basically a good person. I once had a man tell me he did not need the church. After all, he

was a good, moral person. He did good deeds on his own. So why should he be a church member—what did it have for him? Already you can see part of the fallacy in the logic of this statement by reading the other reasons in this epistle for church membership. Being a good, moral person is not enough. And who of us is really, if we are honest, that good?[5] Surely what I can do as an individual by way of "good deeds" for other people in no way compares to what can be done as a body in Christ. No organization in history has ever even begun to hold a candle to the church in service.[6] Harry Emerson Fosdick truly said:

> The church can be to you not only an inspiring fellowship in which your spirit is kindled to new life, but also a challenging opportunity to invest hard work . . . . As Dr. W. E. Sangster said, "I once made a journey around the world. I never once saw 'The Atheists' Home for Orphans,' or 'The Agnostics' Crippleage,' but everywhere I went I saw the Christian Church caring for the destitute and needy."[7]

The church provides a reason and an outlet for service, "good deeds," like no other organization.

(5) *The New Testament plainly tells us to go to church*, just because we are Christians. "Let us not give up meeting together, as some are in the habit of doing, but let us encourage one another—and all the more as you see the Day approaching" *(Hebrews 10:25)*. It also tells us that Jesus regularly attended services, ". . .and on the Sabbath day he went into the **synagogue** as was his custom" *(Luke 4:16)*. You cannot read the Scriptures and fail to realize that the church on earth exists as one of two divinely created institutions. The other is the family. If God created the church for us, who are we to say that we do not need it?

(6) *The church needs you.* If you are a Christian— and a good enough one to see hypocrisy in others—then you can and must help the church become more like Christ. This reminds me of a somewhat amusing conversation (and powerful moral truth) which I had recently with the wife of a minister friend. She was talking about

feelings of righteous indignation she had from an experience, to which I replied, " I long ago stopped having feelings of righteous indignation. I realized that I don't have enough righteousness to be indignant about anything."

The church needs us. It is so much easier to say vaguely that we need a renewal of genuine Christianity in the church. "I'm not going to be a part of a church because I am better than any I know." There is only one place such a renewal can come from—the Christian community, the church!

Can you be a Christian without being a vital part of a local church? You can *become* a Christian without going to a church. But in the final analysis once a person becomes a Christian, he cannot remain in isolation! To me, being a Christian and not being a living part of a church, is much like a person who claims to be a football player without a team. Everywhere he goes people say, "Oh, you are a football player. What team do you play with?" It won't take many times of answering "no team" before people will ask, "Then how can you claim to be a football player?"

There is something inherent in the very idea of being a Christian which demands being a part of a local church. It is absolutely absurd to claim to be a Christian and not be a church member. "Unfortunately many people in the church today are committed to the church as an institution but not committed to Christ as Lord and Savior. You can be committed to the church and not be committed to Christ, but you cannot be committed to Christ without being committed to the church."[8]

I hope this writing finds you an active part of a local church. Wherever you go, one of the very first things you should do is find a new family, God's family—the church! Work to make it the best church it can possibly be with God's help *and* yours!

STUDY/DISCUSSION QUESTIONS

1. Can you be a Christian and not be a member of a church?

2. Why was the church "made" for hypocrites?

3. What should you look for in a church?

4. What *is* the church?

5. Discuss some good reasons for being a member of a local church.

6. What are your responsibilities to the church as a Christian?

FOOTNOTES

[1] See Chapter 8, especially the section "What is Moral Perfection?"

[2] Vernard Eller has written a good book in this regard. *The Outward Bound: Caravaning as the Style of the Church*. Eerdmans, 1980.

[3] I realize that sometimes it seems like a local church cannot be very effectively made into the Church.

[4] Some good books on the church are: F. J. A. Hort, *The Christian Ecclesia*. London: Macmillan, 1914; Han Kung's, *The Church*, New York: Sheed and Ward, 1976; and William Robinson, *The Biblical Doctrine of the Church*. St. Louis: Bethany Press, 1955.

[5] *Ibid.*, Chapter 8.

[6] I know the church has been guilty of much evil, too!

[7] Harry Emerson Fosdick, *Dear Mr. Brown: Letters to a Person Perplexed about Religion*. New York: Harper & Row, 1961, p. 157-8.

[8] Terry L. Miethe, *Reflections*, 1980.

10 / The Meaning of Worship

Worship is one of the most central elements in the life of the Christian, yet it is so misunderstood by so many. In Chapter 9 I said we would look in depth at the question, "What is worship?" This is the first of four short lessons on the subject; e.g., the meaning, nature, purpose, and attitude of worship. In Chapter 9 we said that "worship is an attitude of life." The New Testament Scriptures never speak of a "worship service" or of an "act of worship," or of "special places" in which to assemble to worship, but perhaps this does not mean these are unimportant.[1]

A brief look at the origin of Christian worship is appropriate. Christianity had its background in **Judaism**. In fact, we have retained some of our inherited concept of worship. Jewish types and symbols foreshadowed much that is in Christianity. Paul tells us that "the law was our schoolmaster to bring us to Christ" *(Galatians 3:24)*. There are also great contrasts between Old Testament religion (Judaism) and New Testament religion (Christianity). Jewish worship, though not totally so, was largely formal and ritualistic, adapted to the twelve tribes of Israel.

Christianity, according to the book of Hebrews, is a fulfillment (filling full) of Old Testament Judaism. The following are important differences between the two:

(1) The Jewish high priest offered daily sacrifices for the people. Christ, our High Priest, did this once for all when He did on the cross *(Hebrews 3:1, 7:27)*.

(2) The Jews had animal sacrifices, but Christians believe "only the lamb of God could take away the sins of the world" *(John 1:29)*.

(3) Only Jewish priests could enter the holy place

67

of the **tabernacle**. Every Christian is to worship God —becoming one of a "royal priesthood, a holy nation" *(I Peter 2:9)*, which is the Church. Every Christian is a priest. There is no religious hierarchy in the New Testament.

(4) Judaism was a rather limited national religion. Christianity is for all nations and people *(Matthew 28: 18-20)*.

(5) The Jews kept the **Sabbath** day (Saturday). Christians celebrate on the Lord's Day (Sunday) *and every day of the week!*

So we see there are great differences between Judaism and Christianity.

Many have a very limited concept of worship. They view worship either as only *an* act (church on Sunday) or a feeling. It seems by what these people do, or don't do, during the week that they feel worship is the observance of a prescribed form of ceremony. These people are called "Sunday Christians." Such people, because the once-a-week "worship service" is the essence of their Christianity, get caught up in the form of worship. They follow every detail of order, etc. in the service. If a picture is crooked, or something is moved or done out of place, their "worship" is affected or destroyed. This is a sure sign that the person is a *very* immature Christian no matter what their age. To them the "spirit" of worship is secondary or unimportant.

The New Testament recognizes both aspects of worship. We are told to worship God "in spirit and truth" *(John 4:19-26)*. In this passage of John, Jesus revealed to the woman that the time had come for the "shadowy" types of both Samaritan and Jewish temple worship to end. It is necessary that one's worship issue from the heart (in spirit). Worship in this new age is to be of an entirely different character—not limited to time or place, or to formal acts *(Romans 1:9, 2:29, and Philippians 3:3)*.

The meaning of "in truth" (when compared with other passages where it occurs) seems most probably to be either "in reality," as opposed to the symbolic nature of temple worship, or "in sincerity," in contrast to the formalistic and often pretentious character of Jewish observance. The "vain worship" spoken of in Matthew 15:4-9 is not so much people performing wrong acts as living in rebellion to God's moral law by teaching their own prejudices and petty opinions as God's truth.

There are several words used in the Greek New Testament for worship. Perhaps we can get a better idea of the meaning of worship by looking at them:

(1) *Leiturgia* — "Liturgy" occurs infrequently in the New Testament and not in its modern sense. For this reason it is not found in most English translations of the Bible. It means basically "service" and can refer to service of any kind *(II Corinthians 9:12)*.

(2) Threskeia — "Religion". The Greek dictionary definitions of this word relate it to the "external ceremonies of religious worship." Its scarcity in the New Testament supports the view that Christian worship is not expressed primarily in outward ceremonies *(Colossians 2:18)*.

(3) *Sebomai* is used commonly for the idea of piety. It means to revere, venerate, feel awe and has to do with the spirit of worship *(Matthew 15:9 and Mark 7:7, Acts 13:43, 17:17)*.

4. *Prosuneo* — "Worship" means to prostrate oneself before any person or god, to do him honor, "to bow down." It is mainly used in the Gospels *(Matthew 2:11, 4:9)* and Revelation. Of the 18 occurrences of this word in Matthew, Mark and Luke, 13 refer to people falling prostrate before Jesus.

(5) *Latreuo* — "Worship" means to serve, to work, to labor. In every instance that this word occurs, it describes either the worship and/or service offered to God *(Acts 7:42)*. It would seem that this word is used in a specific way to describe worship that is demonstrated in some definite act of service. *Lateria* finds its highest expression in Romans 12:1. This serves as the best definition of Christian worship; i.e., the offering of yourself as a living sacrifice, holy and acceptable to God—this is rational worship!

In studying the uses and meanings of the various words for worship, I am inclined to agree with a famous Bible scholar who said:

70

The worship of God is nowhere defined in Scripture. A consideration. . .shows that it is not confined to praise; broadly it may be regarded as the direct acknowledgement of God, of His nature, attributes, ways and claims, whether by the outgoing of the heart in praise and thanksgiving or by deed done in such acknowledgement. No one word seems to emerge as "the word" to describe a distinctly Christian form of worship. No act or acts are designated as "the acts of worship." So as far as the language is concerned worship is left in the realm of freedom of expression as the worshipper finds himself/herself in the presence of God. The important point to remember is that God is the active agent in all worship. It is also important to remember that worship is both private and done as a member of the family of God with other family members. It is life itself!

What then is the meaning of worship? Perhaps it can best be put thus: It is a feeling of adoration to God that expresses itself in a life of service to Him! It is a subjective feeling given an objective expression. We need to realize that the meaning of worship for the Christian is praising and serving God in all of life's tasks with all of life's energies. As Christians we need to do this by stirring "up one another to love and good works" and "encouraging one another" (Hebrews 10:24-25). It is my hope and prayer that this is what we do with each other on Sunday and every day of our lives!

STUDY/DISCUSSION QUESTIONS

1. Discuss what it means to say that "worship is an attitude of life."
2. Compare and contrast Judaism and Christianity.
3. Why do some people have such "a very limited concept of worship"?
4. What does it mean to your life to worship God "in spirit and truth" (John 4:19-26)?
5. Discuss how the words used in the New Testament for worship help us to understand it better.
6. Discuss "the meaning of worship" as it relates to your life.

FOOTNOTES

[1]As frail human beings we probably need services, acts, and maybe even special places to help with our worship. But it is a horrible thing when the services, acts and, yes, even places become the main point of worship —more important than living for and serving God!

11 / The Nature of Worship

The last chapter discussed the meaning of worship. I said worship was "a feeling of adoration to God that expressed itself in a life of service to Him." Christians must be taught that worship means a lifelong attitude of praise and service to God. We dare not confuse a "worship service" with true worship. While such a service *can* be worship, it should in no way be thought of as the totality of what constitutes worship.

The "nature" of something is "the inherent character or basic constitution of a thing, the essence." The word "nature" is also used as: "A creative and controlling force in the universe," sometimes referred to as "Mother Nature." Christians know "The Force" in the universe is God! So ultimately God is the inherent character, basic constitution, the creative and controlling force of our worship. God is supreme and yet personal. This has many implications to the nature of worship for us as Christians.

(1) **Christian worship involves and shapes the whole life** *(Matthew 22:36-40)*. Verse 37 of this passage in Matthew comes originally from Deuteronomy 6:4-9. This Old Testament passage is also quoted in Mark *(12:28-34)* and Luke *(10:25-28)* as well. Even in the Old Testament it was God's desire that every aspect of our lives be lived for Him in His presence. We see clearly in the Deuteronomy passage that worship is to permeate every part of life. There are no more "things holy" and "things **secular**." One of the worst evils of our modern world is this false division between "sacred" and "secular!" It has great effects on the church and the ministry which we will discuss in a later letter.

Every realm of life is holy, made so by our acceptance of Christ as Lord and Savior, and by the presence of the Holy

Spirit. Viewed in this way all labor takes on new meaning and character. No matter what our "job," the way we support our families, work can be carried on with character, dedicated to God. Our attitude makes all the difference as to whether the work we do is worship and meaningful. Thus, any labor, unless it is in and of itself unchristian, should be done with dignity, pride, and to the very best of our ability. Remember again Romans 12:1! As Christians, worship is the lifelong process of "presenting our bodies," our very lives "as a living sacrifice, holy, acceptable to God." This is your reasonable service or *worship*.

(2) **Christian worship is for all humankind.** It is universal! It is not just for Abraham's descendants (the Jews), but for all who will acknowledge God and His Son. This universality of the nature of Christian worship is very important. It means that all can become members of God's chosen nation, all can have honor and dignity in life.

(3) **Christian worship is corporate.** What, on this earth, could be more beautiful than the fellowship which can, indeed must, take place within the body of Christ *(I Corinthians 12:12-30)*. When we are made new in Christ, we become, all of us, one in Him! We will have different tasks to do, but we all partake as part of the same family working together toward a shared goal: "that the world may know Him, and through Him have eternal life." How could we possibly be one in Him, united by His love, and not want to share together our lives of worship? Yes, worship is corporate.

(4) **Yet, Christian worship is individual.** The Scripture says, "Let a man examine himself" *(I Corinthians 11:28)*. Each of us, as individuals, will have to answer to God for how we live our lives. I am responsible for how well I use the talents and abilities God has given me, and you are for yours. I will not have to answer for you, nor you for me. I will not be your judge (praise God), nor you mine! Christian worship sweeps away every barrier and brings us together, our lives and spirits, into direct communion with God, who is the object of our worship. If this is not your experience in worship. then look first inside to see if you are open, loving, sharing — then find others who want in turn to share their love and lives in Christ. Perhaps you are not really participating in worship, but only observing others.

(5) **The object of worship is God.** We all have (at least in the past had) idols! Anything, yes *anything*, that is more important to us than God, that we seek after more than God, is an idol! It can be very obvious or very subtle. Money, possessions, power can be idols; so can education, good looks, and even family! The Bible tells us we should be "turned from idols to serve the true and living God" *(I Thessalonians 1:9-10)*.

Our God is a living God, a living personality, with intellectual and spiritual manifestations and faculties. We can relate to God personally! We are told to address God as "our Father" *(Luke 11:1-4)*.

The Nature of Christian worship? The essence of it is God and how we are relating to Him in our lives of worship. It must involve our whole lives. It is for all people. It is corporate *and* individual. We have individual responsibility for our lives and also responsibility to share it with others. And our God, who is the essence of worship, is the object of it!

May each of us have a realization of true worship, a determination and dedication to experience the nature of worship daily in our lives and with others.

STUDY/DISCUSSION QUESTIONS

1. In what ways can worship "involve and shape the whole life" *(Matthew 27:36-40)*?

2. How can you relate your job to a life of worship?

3. Can we make corporate worship more meaningful and enriching to ourselves and others?

4. How can you feel like more of a participant in corporate worship services?

12 / The Purpose of Worship

The previous two discussions were on the "meaning" and "nature" of Christian worship. This one is about the "purpose" of worship. The word "purpose" is defined as: "something set up as an object or end to be attained" and "to propose as an aim to oneself." When discussing the "purpose of worship" we are considering the question, "What is the goal toward which Christians direct their efforts or service to God?"

As a student, and professor of **philosophy**, I learned that one way to get an idea about what something is, is to first inquire as to what it is not.[1] Knowing what something is not will help point us in the correct direction to what it really is. The purpose of worship is *not* **aesthetic** enjoyment. "Such a beautiful service!" "I enjoyed it so much." Is this worship? I am terribly afraid some Christians are so concerned about the mechanics of the worship service (is this or that done correctly) that they cannot praise or serve our God. This condition is aggravated by the fact that many Christians become so comfortable in their faith (not challenged to grow) they lose sight of the true *nature* and *purpose* of Christianity.

Carnegie Samuel Calian, in his excellent book, *Today's Pastor in Tomorrow's World*, says:

> It appears that today's believer is more in search of comfort than adventure. We view our faith as a cautious life insurance policy. It is almost as if our faith has become security-centered rather than Christ-centered. As a result, our actions illustrate a sense of withdrawal, a lack of creativity, daring, and boldness . . . . The Christian life is a matter of continued growth. Christians are not to evade the challenges, struggles, difficulties, and dangers of life, but to confront and deal with them.[2]

Legions have lost sight of the revolutionary nature of Christianity! Becoming so concerned about the outward form of their religion, they have forgotten *who* it is that *we* are to share, *what* we are to share, or even *that* we are to share. Concerned so with trivia, the church sometimes never bothers to share our Lord and His love with others.

Some come to the meeting-house (church) to listen (to sit on the sidelines), others go to worship (to participate). Aesthetic pleasure is not the same as the joy of worship! In planning for "worship service," do not seek *merely* to arouse and please the senses. To seek, in worship, the correctness of form (whatever that is) or the beauty of the surroundings, may be to accept a substitute for worship.

What is joy? Joy is . . . God in us! C. S. Lewis says in his spiritual autobiography, *Surprised by Joy:*

> I had hoped that the heart of reality (regarding Joy) might be of such a kind that we can best symbolize it as a place; instead, I found it to be a Person.[3]

We must realize that the only way we will have joy "in worship" is if we have joy inside. St. Augustine said in 400 A.D., "Indeed the happy life is joy arising from truth."[4]

We will not have joy in life, in worship, unless we *discipline* ourselves to: (1) study God's Word to mature in the Christian life; (2) develop a vital prayer life; (3) be an active participant in worship (an attitude of life); (4) strive to live a Christian life moment by moment (that is all we have to worry about); i.e., develop a God consciousness, share our faith with others.

There are ways to enhance joy, even in worship services, as we take an active part (which, of course, assumes discipline): Give attention to the words of the hymns; pray, in your mind, the words of the prayers; read along in your Bible the words of the Scripture, etc. Become a good listener! You must be willing to let the service, sermon, etc., speak to you—take at least brief notes.

We must realize that *we* set the tone of worship services, each of us as individuals, for ourselves and others. Respond openly and honestly to your experiences: say "amen," clap (occasionally), express warmth to one another (*physically*; e.g., hold hands, "the holy kiss"[5], hug; *verbally*, e.g., "I love you"; *facially*, don't be a prune face!) There are *too many* people in every church who do precious little more than sit back and criticize! I call them "resident experts." They are not willing to roll up their sleeves and get involved in doing a ministry for their church, but *boy!* can they criticize. We will have joy-filled worship services only when we are joy-filled people. Joy . . . must truly be an expression of God in us!

The nature of worship indicates its aim or purpose. We have said this before: "Worship involves the whole of life!" This cannot be over-stressed. It is one of the cardinal truths of Christianity. Many Christians are still living in the days of the Civil War as far as their commitment to Christ and the church is concerned. If you didn't want to serve in the war, and your family had enough money, you could hire someone to fight in your place. This is exactly how numerous Christians today view their pastor. Oh, they probably would never admit it, but their pastor is hired to be a Christian, "to fight the good fight" *(I Timothy 6:12,19)* for them. Again Calian says it well:

> Some, in fact, think it is only the business of ministers and missionaries to live committed lives. G. K. Chesterton, British writer, hinted at this false conclusion in his statement, "People pay ministers to be good, to show the rest of us it doesn't pay to be good." Fortunately, facts prove otherwise. The biblical witness of Christ is universal and inclusive. Yet only a few see themselves as pilgrims, while the majority of us have a settler's mentality. A pilgrim from the viewpoint of the majority is a fanatic, and who among us wants that label? *Yet the obvious fact is that many of us have already become fanatics in our search for other goals outside of Christ* (italics mine). As a result, we have become hesitant pilgrims as Christians. The church as a consequence is filled with hesitant pilgrims suffering from an identity crisis.[61]

Worship is for "the perfecting of the saints" *(Ephesians 4:12)*.

Worship has a four-fold purpose: (1) **Christian worship is to glorify God.** This is the first and foremost aim of Christian worship, one we must never forget. When it's all said, the ultimate aim of worship is to give praise and honor to God. If more Christians realized this, they would be much less critical of "worship services" and much more concerned about their attitudes and lives *(Romans 6:17-18)*. It is *your* attitude which makes life worship or not!

(2) **Worship enables us to grow in grace.** Through worship, as we practice it repeatedly day by day, we are sustained and strengthened in the Christian life *(Ephesians 3:16-21)*. This is one clear reason why worship for one or two hours, once a week, is so very inadequate. When we are in the process of conforming our daily lives to God's will (this is worship), then our faith is not only maintained, but made stronger. In this case the reverse is also *very* true. We starve to death when we "try" to survive as Christians on an hour "worship service"! Corporate worship not only helps us, but others grow in grace *(I Corinthians 10:14-17)*. In worshipping together, we share a common "cup of blessing."

(3) **Worship helps us realize that the presenting of our lives is our offering to God** *(Romans 12:1-2, again)*. "It is no longer I that live, but Christ that lives in me" *(Galatians 2:20)*. Week after week I see so many Christians who are not really dedicated to Christ. They are, at best, only passive observers. How my heart aches for them! Why can't they realize that God's way is "not a way of life, but life itself." Why don't they claim the promises of God? How can they be content to only exist (and not live)?

You must not be like this! You must start today, this very minute, to conform your attitudes, your very being, to allow yourselves to be transformed by Christ. Experience His love and reach out with it to others. Let your life swell up with the joy of having Him live in you.

(4) **The purpose of Christian worship is to spread God's Presence in our world.** Yes, even worship demands evangelism, in both action and word! How could we possibly experience "joy, God in us," and not share that with others *both* in and out of the church.

And we have help to accomplish these aims, these divine purposes in life. We have Christ's presence and His promises *(Matthew 28:20)*, if we will only find out what they are and claim them. We have the gift of the Holy Spirit, if we will only understand and accept it *(Acts 2:38, I Corinthians 3:16)*. Worship itself helps to accomplish its purpose through the church and fellowship, if we are not just passively connected to God's family.

I hope this discussion finds you experiencing the joy and purpose of worship as you blossom in faith and work.

STUDY/DISCUSSION QUESTIONS

1. Is the church you know best overly concerned about the mechanics of worship?

2. How can a spirit of "creativity, daring, and boldness" be put back in our worship?

3. Discuss the ways you can have joy in life, in worship.

4. Why is it important for each of us as individuals to help set the tone for the worship service?

5. Discuss the purpose of worship.

6. How can you relate Christian worship and evangelism?

FOOTNOTES

[1] In theology this is called the "via negativa" and was a method in St. Thomas Aquinas's philosophy/theology.

[2] Carnegie Samuel Calian, *Today's Pastor in Tomorrow's World*, New York: Hawthorn Books, Inc., 1977, p. 72.

[3] C. S. Lewis, *Surprised by Joy: The Shape of My Early Life*, New York: Harcourt, Brace & World, Inc., 1955, p. 230.

[4] Augustine, *Confessions* x, 23. "Beata quippe vita est guadium de veritate," in the Latin.

[5] There are rather frequent expressions of greeting fellow Christians with "the holy kiss" in Scripture; e.g. Romans 16:16, I Corinthians 16: 20, II Corinthians 13:12, I Thessalonians 5:26, and I Peter 5:14.

[6] Calian, Ibid., p. 75.

13 / The Attitude of Worship

This, the last chapter in this series of four, is on the "attitude" of worship. In the *first* discourse on worship I said its "meaning" is best put: "It is a feeling of adoration to God that expresses itself in a life of service to Him." The *second* in the series said of the "nature" of Christian worship: it involves the whole life, it is for all humankind, it is corporate, yet individual, and God is the essence and object of worship. The "purpose" of worship (its aim) was discussed in number *three* of this series. Christian worship is to glorify God, it enables us to grow in grace, it helps us realize that presenting our lives is our offering to God, and worship should help spread God's Presence (influence) in our world!

Assembling on Sunday morning may or may not be worship (depending on our attitudes, etc.). But one thing is certain: This Sunday gathering *cannot* be worship when that is the only worship activity we engage in during the week. True worship must be a daily, almost moment by moment, expression of praise and service to God. If our lives do not reflect this in our very attitude of existence, then certainly "church service" will not be worship for us!

Perhaps we even look at a "church service" in the wrong way. One part of the meeting on Sunday is commonly referred to as "the worship service." Instead of viewing such a service as worship, maybe it would be wise if we made a formal distinction between "worship" (an attitude of life) and assembly (a gathering of people). Then we would realize that Christians meet together not so much for "worship" as to encourage each other in lives that *are* sacrificial worship. Such meetings cannot be viewed as optional! They are essential to the maintenance of Christian faith.

The "atmosphere" of Christian assembly is to be characterized by those same qualities that should govern daily personal relationships among Christians.

(1) "Let no one seek his own good, but that of his
neighbor" *(I Corinthians 10:23 and Philippians
2:1-4).*

(2) "So then let us pursue the things which make for
peace and the building up of one another" *(Romans
14:19).*

(3) "Let each of us please his neighbor for his good, to
his edification" *(Romans 15:2).*

(4) "Do nothing from selfishness or empty conceit, but
with humility of mind let each of you regard one
another as more important than himself" *(Philippians 2:3).*

This is just what the Corinthians were not doing. This is the
problem Paul deals with in I Corinthians, especially chapters
11-14. As John says: "If someone says, 'I love God,' and
hates his brother he is a liar; for the one who does not love his
brother whom he has seen, cannot love God whom he has not
seen" *(I John 4:20).* The Christian Assembly should provide a
format for the expression of mutual love and concern!

One of the central aims of Christians when they met in
assembly in the New Testament was edification *(I Corinthians
14:26* — "edify" is "to instruct and improve especially in moral
and religious knowledge"). It should be characterized by an atmosphere of love, joy, and fellowship. It should "stimulate one
another to love and good works" and "encourage one
another" *(Hebrews 10:24-25).* Many Scriptures speak about
the importance of edification. Here are two more examples:

(1) "And we proclaim Him, admonishing every man
and teaching every man in all wisdom, that we may
present every man complete in Christ" *(Colossians
1:28).*

(2) "Let the word of Christ dwell in you richly, as you
teach and admonish one another in all wisdom"
(Colossians 3:16).

I cannot overstate the importance of your attitude in worship *and* assembly. In both, one should strive to be at their highest and best. If the heart is full of envy, resentment, jealousy, hatred, malice, we cannot worship! These attitudes are at war with every principle of Christian worship. So, too, one cannot worship if they are so uptight, stress-filled that they are running around like "chickens with their heads cut off." I see this often before and during church services. "As a man thinks in his heart, so is he" *(Proverbs 23:7)*.

Unfortunately (believe it or not) some people come to assembly (church services) more to be seen, than to engage in worship. Jesus makes frequent condemnation of such people: "Beware of practicing your righteousness before men to be noticed by them" *(Matthew 6:1)*, "And when you pray" don't do it like the hypocrites, "for they love to stand and pray in the synagogues. . .in order to be seen by men. . ." Matthew 6:5).

Not many commands regarding attitude are given, but principles abound. Obviously (as we have already mentioned), some attitudes are in harmony with worship and assembly, while others are **antithetical**. "Two men went up to the temple to pray" *(Luke 18:11-14)*, one had a *very* self-righteous attitude, one was *very* humble! We are told that an unforgiving spirit prevents true worship *(Matthew 6:12, 5:21-24)*. We are told to "think on these things" *(Galatians 5:22-25)*, the fruit of the Spirit!

The attitude of reverence is an important one in worship and assembly. We are told to "serve God acceptably with reverence and Godly fear" *(Hebrews 12:28)*. We need to take time to meditate upon the majesty and goodness of God. There are several ways mentioned in the New Testament in which we may glorify God in our lives:

(1) Confessing Christ glorifies God. *(Philippians 2:11)*

(2) Bearing "much fruit" glorifies God. *(John 15:8)*

(3) Preaching and spreading the gospel glorify God. *(Galatians 1:24, II Corinthians 4:15)*

(4) Our generosity glorifies God. *(II Corinthians 9:11-13)*

(5) Our spiritual growth glorifies God. *(Philippians 1:9-11)*

Yes, worship and assembly should be characterized by an atmosphere of love, joy, and fellowship. They should provide for witness and evangelism. We *do* have "a story to tell to the nations" (the title of an old hymn). But the nations will only listen if *we* are filled with proper attitudes, if our lives express worship, and if *we* "have this attitude in (ourselves) which was also in Christ Jesus" *(Philippians 2:5)!*

STUDY/DISCUSSION QUESTIONS

1.   Why is "attitude" important to worship?

2.   What is the distinction between "worship" and "assembly"?

3.   Discuss the importance of an "atmosphere" of love in the Christian assembly.

4.   What does it mean to be "edified" in a worship service?

5.   How do *you* glorify God with your life?

14 / On Prayer

Previous articles have touched on the subject of prayer in passing. "Prayer is basically a conversation with God. Remember, you can talk to God anytime." Prayer is a dialogue between God and man. Because prayer is conversation, it implies that you can talk to God about anything, anytime. Because prayer is dialogue, it is *two-way* communication: us to God and God to us. I suggested you "begin and end every day with prayer," and that you "set aside a time each day for solitude; i.e., private prayer or meditation." I have indicated that prayer can be considered a constant process, a life-style (*I Thessalonians 5:15-18*—"pray without ceasing"). "I was constantly thinking about living for Him. It was as if my need to live for Him had been burned into the front of my mind."

Certainly prayer is very important to the Christian. Yet in some ways it is the most elusive of the subjects we have discussed. I am rather positive that no human has all the answers with regard to prayer. This chapter, even more than the others, should be considered introductory. It is not complete nor comprehensive! If you want to become an "expert" on prayer, I suggest you try praying, that is: communicating with God in every way that helps you grow. I also suggest it might be helpful, if you want to learn about prayer, to read almost everything you can find on the subject. You will soon be able to sift through what seems important and helpful.

Before we go on, a word of warning is called for here. To a great degree, prayer is individual. It has all of the characteristics of conversation. It is also subjective (personal and internal). But prayer is not mystical. Just how we communicate with God and God with us is a very difficult question. I personally believe God speaks to us in many ways. He certainly is not limited to our understanding of Him or His ways. He does not have to communicate with every person exactly the way He communicates to us. I believe God communicates to us in at least the following ways: (1) through Jesus in the context of Scripture (by the Living Word through the written word); (2) through the Body of Christ, the Church; (3) other individuals; (4) nature; (5) through the Holy Spirit; and (6) our minds.

We live in an age with many strange people. I have come across numerous people who think God speaks to them in some rather unbelievable ways *and* says very unbelievable things; e.g., that they will be the next "chief of state" of America and savior of the world, they can live with this woman or that, have a license to kill, etc. Often we see on television news or in the papers that someone has killed others and then themselves on what they claimed were orders from God. Not too long ago parents threw each of their several children off a hotel balcony, then jumped to their deaths, because God told them to do this. These things are not of God! The Christian Church down through history has always believed that individual opinion and interpretation should be checked and balanced by Scripture (according to the best **exegetical** method) and by the community of believers; i.e., the Church. Certainly *your* "communication from God" will not contradict Scripture nor is it very likely to go against the wisdom of the Believing Community as it lives and learns in the shadow of Scripture.

One of the most asked questions is, "Why doesn't God answer my prayers? I have prayed so hard and for so many years, but no answer." Some theologians think God answers *every* prayer; e.g., "No," "Wait," or "Yes." I think many times our prayers seem to fail for at least *eight* reasons:

(1) We do not really ask in faith *(James 1:1-9)*.

(2) Many times our prayers are for things that are purely selfish *(James 4:2,3)*. We are not really concerned whether what we are asking is good for us or not. We expect God to be a Celestial Bellhop who jumps at our every ring.

(3) We do not really pray wanting "God's will to be done" even though we may say the words. Even Jesus said, "Your will be done" when He prayed to His Father *(Luke 22:42)*.

(4) We are often impatient. Unless God meets our time-table, He has not answered.

(5) Sometimes we are dishonest when we ask. We are pretending to be what we are not!

(6) More often we ask in ignorance. We just don't know Scripture well enough, or we assume our "right" answer is consistent with God's plan.

(7) We pray in an unforgiving spirit, thinking we are better or holier than others.

(8) We forget another's free will when we pray for our neighbor. Prayer is not coercive upon God nor upon the other person for whom we are praying!

Prayer must never be thought of as some magical way of getting what we are after: a job, money, a certain boy/girl friend, etc. Prayer is "not so much getting what you want as asking God to give you what He wants." I believe one of the main points of prayer is that God wants us to learn to depend on Him and to mature to the place where our needs and wishes are in tune with His will.

Prayer should involve us completely: mind, emotion, **will**. We should use our minds to try to understand God's truth revealed to us. We have a responsibility to do what we can in any given situation to seek out the help of Scripture and Christian friends. Certainly we must concentrate as fully as we can when we are talking to God. We should use our emotions when we pray to help us relate to God. God speaks to the total person! We should use our will (mental powers, volition) when we pray (Romans 15:30).

Martin Luther, A Simple Way to Pray, for a Good Friend, written to his barber, said:

As the saying goes: he who thinks of many things thinks of nothing and accomplishes no good. How much more must prayer possess the heart exclusively and completely if it is to be good prayer!

Luther, a former Catholic priest, was very much against "heaping up empty phrases" (Matthew 6:7) or vain (meaningless) repetition. He called it zerklappern which actually means "to rattle something to pieces." Prayer "is not just petitioning, reciting and speaking. It is learning, meditating, searching and thus acquiring the perspective of eternity."

The disciples of Jesus once asked Him to teach them how to pray *(Luke 11:1)*. His response, called "The Lord's Prayer," is given in Matthew 6:9-13 and Luke 11:2-4. Many churches recite this prayer in unison during services, but what the Lord probably intended was that this be a model for prayer. Here Jesus gave some specific instructions about prayer, indicating its proper spirit, nature, purpose, and content.

> Our Father in heaven, hallowed by your name, your kingdom come, your will be done on earth as it is in heaven. Give us this day our daily bread. Forgive us our debts, as we also have forgiven our debtors. And lead us not into the temptation, but deliver us from the evil one. (The clause "For yours is the kingdom and the power and the glory forever, Amen" is not in the earliest manuscripts.)

The Lord's Prayer tells us some important concerns:

(1) Prayer should consist of praise (adoration) to God. "Our Father in heaven, hallowed (honored, loved) be your name . . ."

(2) In prayer we should be concerned that man's city become God's city. There is a basic outline of God's kingdom: a civilization where brotherhood, compassion, love between people and nations abound! "your kingdom come . . ."

(3) We should be praying (in action and words) that God's will, His way, becomes our mark as individuals and the mark of our society. *We* must reach out in helpfulness and love so that others may become more loving. We must not do things that perpetuate prejudice, argument, anger, or war so that our society will not. "your will be done on earth as it is in heaven . . ."

(4) We can pray for our specific daily physical needs. "Give us this day our daily bread . . ."

(5) Prayer for forgiveness of our sins, our shortcomings, is important. "Forgive us our debts . . ."

(6) We should pray about our attitudes. It is pretty clear
     that we will not be forgiven until we are forgiving
     (Matthew 18:21-35)—the parable of the unforgiving
     servant). "as we also have forgiven our debtors . . ."

(7) We should pray for the leadership of the Holy Spirit
     in everyday life. "And lead us not into temptation,
     but deliver us from the evil one."

Much, much, much more could be said on the important
subject of prayer *(Colossians 4:2-6)*. Worship, adoration,
praise, **communion**, thanksgiving, confession, petition, inter-
cession (prayer for another), and commitment all belong to prayer
as described in the New Testament.[1] But I will close with two final
thoughts. Thomas R. Kelly, *A Testament of Devotion*, again points
us to an important spiritual truth when he says:

> But behind the scenes, *keep up the life of simple prayer
> and inward worship. Keep it up throughout the day.*
> (italics mine) Let inward prayer be your last act before
> you fall asleep and the first act when you awake. (p. 28)

One of my most favorite prayers is by Phillip Brooks. I
commend it to you:

> Do not pray for easy lives; pray to be stronger men. Do
> not pray for tasks equal to your powers; pray for powers
> equal to your tasks. Then the doing of your work will be
> no miracle. But you yourself shall be a miracle. Everyday
> you shall wonder at yourself, at the richness of life which
> has come to you by the grace of God.

STUDY/DISCUSSION QUESTIONS

1. What is "prayer"?

2. How does God communicate to you?

3. Discuss the importance of a check and balance in regard to what an individual believes to be God communicating with them?

4. Why doesn't God answer prayers?

5. What does it mean to live a life of prayer?

6. Jesus' prayer, called The Lord's Prayer, is intended to be a model for prayer. Discuss how.

7. How can you make Phillip Brooks' prayer a part of your life?

FOOTNOTES

[1]We see the example of Jesus in prayer in John the seventeenth chapter where he prays for Himself (1-5), for His disciples (6-19), and for all believers (20-26).

15 / Fellowship in Christ

This discourse is about Christian fellowship, one of the most important, and yet ignored, essentials of the Christian life. The church lacks great power today precisely because it has not understood or maximized the potential of fellowship. There are many reasons for this: (1) the selfishness of our age; (2) insecurity; (3) jealousy; (4) immaturity; (5) ignorance; and (6) laziness, to mention a few. It takes much effort and dedication of time to build real commitment to one another as brothers and sisters in Christ. We live in an age of shallow commitments and relationships! This is seen on every hand and certainly in marriage and in the church. This may yet be the death of our civilization as we know it.

Christians (of all individuals) and the church (of all institutions) should be a glowing source of intimacy. Yet often we see more commitment and concern expressed in social and sports clubs than in our churches. People no longer think first of a church to find acceptance and love, a sense of real belonging. What a tragedy! You *cannot* be a maturing Christian and not care for and be reaching out to other people intentionally and continually.

In any generation if we, as Christians, are to lead and/or impact the society in which we live, we must be willing to: (1) be radically committed to God, have an extreme God consciousness. Christians must realize their self-worth and very being comes from knowledge and experience of God. And (2) we must form intimate communities in which we live in loving relationship to one another and not as individuals caught up in personal priorities *(Philippians 2:20-21)*, prejudice, or petty ego. Can we really be Christians and only casually committed to each other and to the church? I think not.

As Christians, we need to light the fires of fellowship anew in our lives and in the lives of others!

The Meaning of Fellowship:

Kittel's *Theological Dictionary of the New Testament* defines *koinos* as "of the religious communism of love," and that it "is a spontaneous expression of the disposition of love created by Christ and the Spirit." *(Acts 4:32)* The Greek word *koinonos* means "fellow," "participant." "Hence the word is especially adapted to express inner relationship. "[1]

The fundamental connotation of the root *koin-* is that of sharing *in* something *with* someone. It is also found in the New Testament in the sense of a willingness to give a share; hence the meaning generosity. We have a share in Christian work *(II Corinthians 8:32)*. We give a share as Christians when we contribute freely of ourselves and our wealth *(II Corinthians 9:13, Romans 15:26)*. *Koinonia* (fellowship) described the spiritual bond which joined the early Christians and which expressed itself in the outward acts of pooling material resources. The church must be constantly about sharing *(Acts 2:42, I John 1:3-4)*.

Fellowship with God:

Christians believe in God's Divine Self-disclosure; i.e., God revealed Himself to humankind. This is called "revelation." God reveals Himself to us in many ways though chiefly through the Bible, nature, and other believers. But what is the purpose of "revelation"? William Robinson says it well:

> In the Bible it is just as foreign to ask whether a man can be a Christian without being a member of the Christian Church as it is to ask whether a man can be a Jew without belonging to the Israel of God. This is so because the church is the *fellowship* (koinonia), and the whole work of creation and redemption—God's activity on and within the historical plane—is just God's bid for fellowship with man. And this creative and redemptive activity of God is what the Bible means by 'revelation.' *(Heb. galah; Gr. apocalypsis)*[2]

Thus we miss the mark if we do not see the doctrines of creation and redemption in personal terms.[3] For the believer one of the greatest teachings of Christianity is the possibility of fellowship with a personal God. Even in the Old Testament the **Israelites** saw **Yahweh** as a personal, living God.[4] To realize the striking contrast this presents with many other religions is to understand much of the Judeo-Christian religion!

Such fellowship is a complete contradiction of all forms of pantheistic mysticism, which teach the absorption of the individual in the World-soul and talk of 'A shoreless, soundless sea, Wherein at last our souls must fall.'[5]

Fellowship, its possibility with God and other people because we are created in God's image, becomes the hidden structure of reality. Fellowship is, therefore, essential to life in any meaningful sense, both with God and humankind. This is the very purpose of revelation.

Fellowship with Christ:

Christians have their clearest example of fellowship in the life of Jesus. He taught His disciples not only formally, but openly, by example in lived fellowship. They lived together in a group! Here was time for close personal relationships in quiet meditation and intimate sharing of personality. Jesus knew that formal abstract teaching was not enough to reveal or adequately express the Kingdom of God. He not only lived "among" us, but He lived as we live *(Romans 8:3)*.[6] Fellowship in Jesus' example was "the nonexplosive interlocking of those rich differences of personality which, if left to themselves or organized on a class basis, would lead to endless strife" *(I Corinthians 1:9-10)*.

The Greek word *koinonia* became filled with new content because Jesus lived, died, and rose to new life. It was in the life, death, and resurrection of Christ that fellowship was reborn to live forever in the hearts of men and women. This is why the church can be called the body of Christ. The church, in its deepest meaning, is now—and forever on earth—the embodiment of divine fellowship. It is our main purpose as Christians (making up the body of Christ, the church) to continually bring witness to the world that the ultimate structure of reality is fellowship: God with us, and each of us with others *(I*

John 1:7). This is really the message of Christianity. This is the very reason God has shared His love and His Son with us *(I John 1:3).*

Fellowship with Each Other:

From the very beginning the early Christians experienced a peculiar sense of unity. Christ is at the center of this unity and is the origin of every expression of fellowship. Fellowship must prevail among us by virtue of the Grace of Christ and the ministry of the Holy Spirit. Some theologians have taught that the most forceful expressions of the idea of fellowship are presented symbolically in the parable of the Vine and the Branches *(John 15:1-14)* or in the figure of the Body and its Members *(Romans 12:4-21, I Corinthians 12:12-25).*

If the church members, by virtue of their being members, are joined to Christ, they are also joined to one another *(Romans 12.5, Ephesians 4:25).* We can bear each other's burdens, confide in each other, help each other live as Christ would have us live, and share ultimate joy! "It is true that no fellowships in the world are so close and inspiring as those in which lives are united in loyal service of Christ, seeking for the 'furtherance of the gospel'."[7]

It is as if Christians are joined physically with the closeness experienced by Siamese twins. Our very life's blood flows from one to another. We can share of our very beings in fellowship with and commitment to Christ! We can only truly exist in relation to each other. We are only complete, whole, in relation to one another. This is *koinonia,* the essence of the church. This is the hidden structure of reality itself to which we must constantly give witness and expression in our world. Be constantly reaching out to others with the Christ in you!

STUDY/DISCUSSION QUESTIONS

1. Why does the church lack "power" or influence today?

2. How can a church maximize the potential for fellowship?

3. Why do you think "we live in an age of shallow commitments and relationships"?

4. As Christians, we must lead and/or impact the society in which we live. How?

5. What does "fellowship" mean?

6. Discuss the meaning of "the possibility of fellowship with a personal God."

7. How is Jesus' life an example to us in fellowship?

8. Why are "unity" and "fellowship" so important to Christians?

FOOTNOTES

[1]Gerhard Kittel, Editor, *Theological Dictionary of the New Testament,* Volume III. Grand Rapids, MI: Wm B. Eerdmans Pub. Co., 1965, p. 789-809.

[2]William Robinson, *The Biblical Doctrine of the Church,* Revised edition. St. Louis, MO: The Bethany Press, 1955, p. 15.

[3]See the chapter: "God's Love For Us" in this volume.

[4]R. T. France, *The Living God.* Downers Grove, IL: Inter Varsity Press, 1970.

[5]Robinson, *Ibid.,* p. 17.

[6]See the chapter: "The Humanity of Christ" in this volume.

[7]Charles R. Erdman, *The Epistle of Paul to the Philippians.* Philadelphia, PA: The Westminster Press, 1966, p. 98.

16 / Christian Stewardship

Stewardship is like so many other Christian teachings: rather easy to define, but much harder to actually accomplish. Reference has been made to Christian stewardship in these chapters; e.g., "If we are truly trying to live for Christ, it will be fairly easy to see. More and more our thoughts, time and energy, our personal and financial resources will be used for Him and His Church."[1] The simplest, most basic definition of Christian stewardship is: "A Christian steward is someone who realizes that *everything* they have and all that they are, every aspect of their being, is a gift given to them by God. Therefore, one who is God's steward tries to use every gift, every talent, every material thing God has *loaned* to him in the most efficient way possible to share God's love with others and to further God's kingdom on earth."

The Meaning of "Stewardship":

The dictionary defines "steward" as "one employed in a large household or estate to manage its domestic concerns." In the Old Testament a steward is a man who is "over a house" *(Genesis 43:19, 44:4, Isaiah 22:15)*. In the New Testament there are two words translated steward: (1) *epitropos (Matthew 20:8, Galatians 4:2)*, a guardian; one to whose care or honor one has been entrusted. And (2) *oikonomos (Luke 16:2,3, I Corinthians 4:1,2, Titus 1:7)*, a manager or superintendent—from *oikos* (house) and *nemo* (to dispense or manage). This word describes delegated responsibility.

The word *oikonomos* is used of the Christian's responsibility which is delegated to him by Christ. All things are Christ's, and as Christians we are His executors or stewards.

Numbers of people have a disappointingly narrow understanding of "stewardship." They always think of "stewardship" as giving money (which they often times do with the wrong attitude—*II Corinthians 9:6-8*). Christ expects us to be stewards of our physical world (ecology), material resources (money, home, etc.), time, body, and mind, etc.! When we realize that the term "good steward" is synonymous with the term "Christian," we are on the road to a mature understanding of our faith.

There isn't much chance for us to grow as individuals or the church to grow until we understand and really desire to be good stewards of all that God has given us. We need to be mindful of our world's resources and use them sparingly. We need to see ourselves as vessels of God whose purpose is to help others so to live. We need to see "giving" not in terms of "our" time or money, but God's. We need to realize that the substantial time and money given is just wise use of God's resources delegated to us. It is God's love, grace, and bounty we share! How can I say it any more plainly? If we belong to God, all that we have, all that we are belongs to Him. Giving in quality and quantity is our nature as Christians. This is stewardship of life. The New Testament is not silent about money, talent, or giving.

Stewardship in the New Testament:

In the New Testament stewardship is always person-centered. Attention is never fixed upon things and money as such. With reference to mankind and material things, Jesus had two basic concerns which are expressed over and over: (1) Mankind should be free from the tyranny of things. If we are being controlled by "things," we cannot be putting God in control of our lives. Freedom from being controlled by things may be found only in submission to the sovereignty of God *(Matthew 6:33)*. We must choose between God and **mammon** (hoarded wealth—*Matthew 6:19-34)*. (2) Jesus taught, with regard to material things, that we should be concerned for the needs of our brothers and sisters. He taught that our attitude toward others reflects our true attitude toward, and relationship to, God. Jesus taught that when we give to others we give to Him *(Matthew 25:31-46)*. Jesus praised the widow who gave two small coins as having given more than did the rich. She gave her very living and they gave only out of an excess.

In the story of the rich farmer *(Luke 12:16-21)*, Jesus tells us about a man who was really controlled by what he thought he owned. The farmer dreamed of more and bigger barns only to be told: "You fool! This very night your soul is required of you; and now who will own what you have prepared?"*(v. 20)*. Jesus warned against living for "treasures" which can be destroyed *(Matthew 6:19-21)*. He says that worry over things is unnecessary *(v. 26)*. He tells us that where our treasure is, there will our hearts be also *(v. 21)*. Jesus climaxed his teaching by commanding that we "seek first His kingdom, and His **righteousness**" *(v. 33)*.

Paul praised the Philippians for sharing with him "in the matter of giving and receiving" *(Philippians 4:15)*. Certainly Paul recognized the importance to fellowship *(koinonia)* of giving and receiving. He quoted Jesus as saying: "It is more blessed to give than to receive" *(Acts 20:35)*. Paul appealed to the Corinthian Christians to give as an expression of their love *(agape)*. Christian giving is the outward sign, a proof of God's love at work in a Christian *(II Corinthians 8:7-9)*. Paul taught that giving was to be generous (liberal) and free *(II Corinthians 9:6-15)*. Giving, whether one is talking about the substance of talents in a life lived or money, should be spontaneous *and* according to deliberate purpose *(v. 7)*. Money, in Paul's view, is neither good nor evil. But the love of money is the root of all evil *(I Timothy 6:10)*.

We have not said anything in this letter about tithing. This is because the New Testament does not teach tithing in relation to giving![2] Tithing, the giving of ten percent off the top, was a requirement in the Old Testament for the Jew *(Malachi 3:10)*. If you have understood this chapter, you realize immediately why tithing is not taught in the New Testament. The standard for giving is *infinitely* higher! Our all—our total being should be our gift! Yet many Christians tithe. They find it a fair beginning place for giving at least in regard to money. I find it is true that the best way to assure regular, planned, sustained giving of financial resources is to "pledge" a certain, definite weekly, monthly amount or percentage. This percentage is between you and God. *You* have to justify it to God, not to me or any other person. You have to justify what you keep, not what percentage you give. Giving, whatever your percentage, to be harmonious with the New Testament, must be rooted in the grace and love of God! ·

Stewardship and Your Life:

You are a bright, shining new creation in Christ's kingdom! Remember it is much easier to start new good habits at the beginning than to try to break old bad ones later on in your Christian life. I believe that there is no substitute for good intelligent planning in all of life. Think through each of these letters and ask yourself how each one speaks to you and how each one is to be applied in your life. How can you best give to God now? What percentage of time, area in regard to talents, amount of money can you give? What goals should you make (a year from now, five years, twenty years from now) as you attempt to mature in your service/stewardship for Christ?

Of course, by now, from reading the previous discourses you see clearly that an "offering," any gift, is an act of worship! You are beginning to see how all of these different subjects really overlap, complement each other in the Christian life. "Stewardship" is a very broad term which describes our responsibility to God in all of life. This is brought into sharp focus every Sunday at the time of offering. This is a time which should remind us (a symbol really) of how we have "offered" our total beings to God in the days past and to think on how we will offer ourselves to Him in days ahead. It is next to meaningless if it is only a time to put a few dollars in a plate!

In using Paul's statement, "now concerning the collection for the saints," *(I Corinthians 16:1a)* to teach stewardship, we have very possibly done him an injustice. Rather, we should have been using his admonition: "present your bodies a living sacrifice" *(Romans 12:1b)*. One is an appeal for contributions to meet a certain need in the church, while the other is a basic principle of the Christian life. The first is only meaningful if it flows out of the second! Both are necessary! The giving of an offering to allow the church to function or to help people in need *and* the dedicating of our lives in praise and service to God are both acts of worship! Please, as Christians, let us do both: live lives of worship which answer specific needs of the church and people. For to do less is really to do neither one.

STUDY/DISCUSSION QUESTIONS

1. What is "the simplest, most basic, definition of Christian stewardship"? How does this apply in life situations?

2. Discuss the concept of stewardship revealed by the New Testament words.

3. Why is an understanding of "stewardship" necessary for a church to grow?

4. "Stewardship is always person-centered in the New Testament." What does this mean?

5. Discuss the story of the rich farmer *(Luke 12:16-21)*. Does it relate to you?

6. Why is it "more blessed to give than to receive" *(Acts 20:35)*?

7. Discuss "tithing" and its importance to the modern church.

8. How can *you* grow in Christian stewardship?

FOOTNOTES

[1]See the chapter: "On Being a Christian" in this volume.

[2]Tithes are mentioned only three times in the New Testament: (1) in condemning the Pharisees as hypocrites because they neglected justice, mercy, and faithfulness while giving meticulous care to the tithing of even garden produce *(Matthew 23:23; Luke 11:45—New American Standard Version)*; (2) in the story of the proud Pharisee who "prayed to himself," and boasted that he fasted twice each week and tithed all his possessions *(Luke 16:12);* and (3) in arguing for the superiority of Melchizedek, and hence of Christ, to Levi *Hebrews 7:6-9)*. But certainly *none* of these passages can be taken in any way to teach that tithing is a "religious" obligation of a Christian.

17 / Ministry and the Christian

Have you ever come across an individual or a group with a rather highly specialized vocabulary and had trouble understanding them? Almost every industry today has such a vocabulary for "insiders" expressed in acronyms[1] or buzz-words[2]. But what if the people who used this specialized vocabulary gradually lost the meaning of its words; no longer understood it, but continued to use it? Well, obviously many problems would result: (1) not much work would be accomplished; (2) certainly communication and knowledge of each other and of their original purpose would be increasingly blurred; (3) **traditions** (routines) would develop in place of understood conceptual content. And, finally, (4) a religious mystical form would develop in the group which allowed it to function, but persons who challenged the status quo had better watch out!

This is exactly what has happened in the church! One of the greatest victories of Satan has been to allow the church to have a high sounding religious vocabulary, but the average member no longer really understands it.[3] "Ministry" is such a word! The concept of "ministry," and who is responsible for it, is definitely one of the most important in Christianity. Yet, like so many other Christian teachings, the "ministry" is greatly misunderstood (intellectually and psychologically) by church members.

The Word "Minister":

In the New Testament the characteristic word for minister is *diakonos*. It means: "one who renders service to another; an attendant, servant" *(Matthew 20:26,22:13; John 2:5,9)*. Anyone who performs a service for or in Christ's name is engaged in Christian ministry. Lowly service is the example of ministry in the New Testament. The greatest of Christians should be a "minister," "servant" to the rest *(Matthew 20:26, Mark 10:43)*.

The lowliness of Christian service is emphasized even more strongly by the use of the word doulos or "slave." Paul tells us that Jesus assumed the form of such a "bond-servant" *(Philippians 2:7)*. Paul called himself, the apostles and their fellow-laborers slaves (bond-servants) of God or Christ *(Romans 1:1, Galatians 1:10, Colossians 4:12, Titus 1:1, James 1:1, II Peter 1:1)*.

Jesus' Example of Ministry:

The pattern of Christian ministry is provided by the life of Christ.[4] He came not to receive service but to give it *(Matthew 20:28)*. Our Lord rejected the world's standards and made the servant role the mark of greatness *(Mark 10:42-45)*. The greatest title which one may receive is not "Master," "Father," "Doctor," or "Teacher"; it is "servant" *(Matthew 23:6-11)*. The verb used in Matthew 20:28 and Mark 10:45 *(diakonein)* suggests something like waiting at a table. It reminds us of when Jesus washed the disciples' feet *(John 13:1-15)*.

The real meaning of ministry for all Christians is service in the world and to one another following the example of our Master. Jesus lived His life rendering humble and loving service to individuals and to humanity at large. Jesus' life, lived on earth for us, provided us with the perfect example of selfless love in a servant's heart! When we serve others we not only serve in Christ's name, but we serve with Him.

Ministry in the New Testament:

There are many passages in the New Testament[5] text of interest in regard to Christians and ministry.[6] The following are a few important examples:

I Peter 2:5,9

. . . you, also, like living stones, are being built into a spiritual house to be a holy priesthood, offering spiritual sacrifices acceptable to God through Jesus Christ . . . you are a chosen people, a royal priesthood, a holy nation, a people belonging to God, that you may declare the praises of him who called you out of darkness into his wonderful light.

The idea of a temple made up of the people of God is found in the New Testament in a number of places; e.g., I Corinthians 3:16. Here in I Peter we have a clear statement of the **priesthood of believers**: (1) Christians are the living Church. The Church can no longer be spoken of in terms of a physical building. (2) We offer "spiritual sacrifices" as priests by giving our lives to God through Jesus Christ. This is worship. (3) Our message as priests is to "declare the praises of Him" who has enlightened us, to extend His call to others.

Romans 12:1,2

Therefore, I urge you, brothers, in view of God's mercy, to offer your bodies as living sacrifices, holy and pleasing to God—which is your spiritual worship. Do not conform any longer to the pattern of this world, but be transformed by the renewing of your mind. Then you will be able to test and approve what God's will is—his good, pleasing and perfect will.

In the New Testament a higher and more spiritual service is to be rendered; not the sacrifice of animals, but the consecration of our whole beings. The believer is rationally to serve God in a lifelong process that involves the whole person. Hodge writes: "It is not the thing offered that is said to be reasonable in the sense of, endowed with reason, but the nature of the service. It is rendered by the mind."[7] We are to undergo a metamorphosis of mind to the purpose of *proving* and *approving* the will of God. This alteration comes about as a constant testing, by the mind, of the data with which it is presented, and a continual re-affirming in its decisions of the will of God, "that which is good, acceptable, and perfect." Thus, our spiritual worship as Christians involves a lifetime of living for Christ and constant mental service, learning, etc.

II Corinthians 5:17-20

Therefore, if anyone is in Christ, he is a new creation; the old has gone, the new has come! . . . that God was reconciling the world to himself in Christ, . . . We are therefore Christ's ambassadors, as though God were making his appeal through us. We implore you on Christ's behalf: Be reconciled to God.

Here we see an important order to the work of priest which is the *privilege* and *duty* of every Christian: (1) every Christian is a new being! (2) God, through Christ, gives to us the ministry of reconciliation. (3) As priests, we have the status of ambassadors (one who speaks with authority for another, not just passive representation) of Christ. This is a very clear message: God has given to individual Christians the very ministry He gave to Christ; i.e., that of spreading the word of love and reunion.

Revelation 1:6, 5:10, 20:6

. . . and has made us to be a kingdom and priests to serve his God and Father . . . . You have made them to be a kingdom and priests to serve our God, and they will reign on the earth . . . but they will be priests of God and of Christ and will reign with him . . . .

These three passages from the book of Revelation tell us that the church is a kingdom of priests commissioned to serve God forever. This is the central doctrine of the priesthood of all believers: All Christians are divinely appointed to be priests. If you are a Christian, you are a priest, that is, minister. Could it be more plain?

Ephesians 4:11-12

It was he who gave some to be apostles, some to be prophets, some to evangelists, and some to be pastors and teachers, to prepare God's people for works of service, so that the body of Christ may be built up . . . .

There is a **"specialized leadership ministry"** in the New Testament. Ephesians 4 is clear: These pastors and teachers have a responsibility to prepare the church for the work of ministry. It is through the service of God's *people* that "the body of Christ" is built up.

It is very evident from each of these passages that: service, ministry, priesthood (greatly overlapping concepts in the New Testament) are to envelop the whole life of every Christian. All of life is made holy. It is the responsibility of every Christian to live out their faith in practical application as he/she serves as a priest of God. This is their role as *Christians*, the very meaning of the word!

Your Life and Ministry:

The ministry of Christ *is* the "vocation" of *every person*, young or old, black or white, man or woman, that comes down the aisle to be buried with Jesus in Christian baptism. When you become a Christian, you become a minister![8] *(Mark 8:34-36)*. To be in Christ is to be a minister of Christ. This cannot be overstated or stated too often. Every Christian is to be doing what, in all too many of our churches, we find only the "clergyman" doing. Yes, you, as "ordinary" members of the church, are required to witness, to tell others the good news of Christ, to call, to live Christ every minute of your lives! There is no distinction in the New Testament between "clergy" and "laity." It is a basic contradiction of terms to call someone who is not performing as a minister a Christian. Francis O. Ayres says it as well as anyone:

> You are a minister of Christ. In all fairness, an exposition of the ministry of the laity has to begin with that statement. If you are a baptized Christian, you are already a minister. Whether you are ordained or not is immaterial. No matter how you react, the statment remains true. You may be surprised, alarmed, pleased, antagonized, suspicious, acquiescent, scornful, or enraged. Nevertheless, you are a minister of Christ.[9]

Because of their personal relationship to Christ, all believers have a direct approach to God and are therefore priests *(I Peter 2:9)*. None needs another to intervene between them and God. Every soul may, and must, stand in personal relationship to God. Carnegie Samuel Calian says:

> Actually, the servant-shepherd model should include all persons who consider themselves among the people of God. In other words, this model is not exclusively limited to the professional clergy. The servant-shepherd model applies to the entire Laos—the people of God. Each member . . . must take seriously the implications of the priesthood of all believers. We have *all* been baptized into a common priesthood. We are all disciples. There are no first—and second—class Christians. We are called upon

> to serve and to celebrate a common ministry. Our Christian vocation is to be servants and shepherds to each other. I think it is a poor theology that nurtures and conditions church people to expect a core of persons to be "selfless servants" and "shepherds" while the remainder of the flock does its own thing—playing Christian when it is convenient.[10]

Indeed, the priesthood of all believers *is* an essential doctrine and important distinctive of the Christian religion!

If it is so clear that the priesthood of all believers is such an important distinctive of Christianity, then why doesn't it seem to work? Several things need to be said to this point:

(1) People follow the path of least resistance. It seems almost "natural" that the average person is not going to do any more than necessary. Certainly an idea like the priesthood of all believers demands much from people who would follow it.

(2) People who work all day at any job may not have the time or energy level necessary to actively engage in ministry at other times.

(3) The secular/sacred distinction in our culture does not lend itself to an understanding of the responsibilities of priesthood.

(4) In theological seminaries and in the local church we give only lip service to this doctrine. In fact some ministers are so insecure about their positions that they do not really encourage priestly participation.

(5) Some churches have misunderstood the doctrine of the priesthood of all believers to mean that because they are free in Christ, they do not have to do anything. Their own thing, after all, is not witnessing or preaching. Preaching is something they pay the preacher to do, etc.

(6) It must be recognized that there will always be a division between the ideal and the practical. It will never be possible to "work out" the idea on any level near perfection.

(7) One might want to argue that the idea of the priesthood of all believers does work. This is why Protestants have always enjoyed more freedom from within

the church. We do not always see the subtle ways that people minister. Much more ministry is going on than it looks like on the surface. It is this kind of unseen ministry that really keeps the church alive from generation to generation.

If people don't want to minister (serve), they will not have any trouble coming up with excuses for why they can't. Just like most people who *claim* to be church members don't have any trouble coming up with reasons for not coming to church or for not really being a living part of its family!

We have spouted a lot of "theory" and general statements, but what of "specifics" and "particulars"? (1) We know, without a doubt, that God wants you to minister, to serve Him and others. (2) He expects you to use the talents He has given you to minister. (3) You should be in training for ministry constantly throughout life (while you are actually, at the same time, serving). The Christian life *must* be one of commitment, dedication, and discipline as you strive to learn and grow in your ability to serve *at every age*. (4) Find someone and some local church you can trust and ask them (beg them, demand) to help you learn what your particular gifts and abilities are and to help you in their use *(Philippians 2:20-22)*.

Brothers and sisters, we are not here talking about something that is tangential[11] to the Christian life. We are talking about the Christian life itself! May God grant you a life full of fruitful ministry for Him and to others!

STUDY/DISCUSSION QUESTIONS

1. Why is it so dangerous to have a "religious vocabulary" but not understand what it means?

2. What does the New Testament word for ministry mean?

3. Discuss the implications of Jesus' example of ministry.

4. Five texts that speak of ministry are listed in this chapter. How do they apply?

5. How are you ministering as a Christian?

6. How can you grow so that you will be better able to minister in the future?

7. What is the "priesthood of all believers"? How can this be made more real in a church?

110

FOOTNOTES

[1]Acronyms are "words formed from the initial letter or letters of each of the successive parts or major parts of compound term"; e.g., REE, Request for Engineering Evaluation.

[2]Buzzwords: "an important-sounding usually technical word or phrase often of little meaning used chiefly to impress laymen."

[3]This is perhaps one of the most powerful reasons why we need very strong Christian education programs today, more than ever.

[4]See the chapter in this volume: "The Humanity of Christ."

[5]Scripture is quoted from the *Greek New Testament* and the *Holy Bible: New International Version*.

[6]These passages are chosen because they are some which most clearly speak to the priesthood of all believers and which have been repeatedly recognized in church history as important to a development of said doctrine. In a discussion of this type, and from a textual analysis, it is obvious that their contextual relationships are not violated. All five of the passages are addressed to specific audiences; e.g., I Peter "to those who reside as aliens, scattered throughout Pontus, Galatia, Cappadocia, Asia, and Bithynia" *(I Peter 1:1)*, to the Christians in Rome *(Romans 1:7)*, to the Christians in "Corinth and throughout Achaia *(II Corinthians 1:1)*, to the seven churches in Asia *(Revelation 1:4)*, and the "saints who are at Ephesus *(Ephesians 1:1)*. It is also obvious from the very beginning of the church that these letters were circulated because it was understood they were also intended for *all* Christians.

[7]Charles Hodge, *Commentary of the Epistle to the Romans*. A. C. Armstrong and Son, 1906, p. 604.

[8]Several good books that stress the importance of this doctrine are: Robert Lowry Calhoun, *God and the Day's Work*. New York: Fleming H. Revell Company, 1943, 81 pages. W. R. Forrester, *Christian Vocation: Studies in Faith and Work*, being the Cunningham Lectures, 1950 in New College, Edinburgh. New York: Charles Scribner's Sons, 1953, 223 pages. Francis O. Ayres, *The Ministry of the Laity: A Biblical Exposition*, Philadelphia, PA: Westminster Press, 1962, 139 pages. Elton Trueblood, *The Company of the Committed*, New York: Harper & Row, 1961, 113 pages. Larry Peabody, *Secular Work is Full-Time Service*, Fort Washington, PA: Christian Literature Crusade, 1974. And Carnegie Samuel Calian, *Today's Pastor in Tomorrow's World*, New York: Hawthorn Books, Inc., 1977, 153 pages.

[9]Ayres, *Ibid.*, p. 25.

[10]Calian, *Ibid.*, p. 10-11.

[11]"2: diverging from an original purpose or course: IRRELEVANT."

18 / Sharing Your Faith

We have established that Christians are supposed to share their faith *(Matthew 28:18-20)*.[1] "Witness" is really another name for "ministry," for "fellowship," for "living the Christian life." The word "witness" in the New Testament is *martyreo* (verb) and compounds *martys, martyria*, and *martyrion*. Our English word "martyr" comes from this Greek one. A "martyr" is one who gives the supreme witness; "one who voluntarily suffers death as the penalty of witnessing to and refusing to renounce his religion" *(Acts 22:20)*. The Christian's proper function, within the world in which we live, is to bear our witness to Him as we go! In the New Testament witnessing is seen to have been both spontaneous and normal, as well as studied and deliberate.

Yet, for many Christians, new ones and older ones as well, "witnessing" about their faith does not come easily. There are many reasons for this:

(1) *Fear that we will get a negative reaction.* We are responsible for the message *and* for presenting it in a loving way. We are not responsible for the reaction! Perhaps the real reason for the fear of a bad reaction is a realization that we have not been consistent, loving, and forgiving enough in our lives. Then, we try to witness in a way which shows us up for what we are.

(2) *Fear that people are going to ask us questions for which we do not know the answer(s).* There is nothing wrong with saying "I simply don't know." In fact, that simple sentence is *frequently* the most intelligent thing *any* individual can say! After you admit you don't have all the answers, tell them you will try to find out if there

is an answer. Then seek help! *If the average Christian realized that part of the very essence of the Christian life is constant disciplined learning[2], the times when one would be caught without some type of answer would be much less often.*

(3) *Feelings of personal inadequacy make us afraid to witness.* We would feel less and less inadequate if we had dedicated our lives to the disciplined study mentioned above! But we must also realize that personal inadequacy is a universal disease. We all suffer from it to some degree. In any generation if we, as Christians, are to impact the society in which we live, we must be willing to be radically committed to God. Christians must realize their self worth and very being comes from God. The more we rely on God (as we labor to understand, to love, and to give), the less personal inadequacy will be our concern!

(4) *We have a misunderstanding of the whole area of witnessing.* We allow people who have given witness a bad name by certain actions to keep us from witnessing at all. "Beating people over the head with the Bible" is *not* witnessing! The Bible was not written for that purpose. It was written so people might have fellowship with God and with each other in Christ. The Bible is seen in miniature in John 3:16. It is a book which reveals God's love for us, how we are to mature in Christ, and (to some extent) the folly of a life apart from God. It is primarily written for believers, not for unbelievers. We should witness to (share with) unbelievers at *their* point of need; e.g., belief in God or the lack of it, need for acceptance, love, meaning and purpose in life, etc.

Often we think of witnessing as showing righteous indignation[3] at a dirty joke or the disagreeable actions of a fellow worker. Thus our "witnessing" becomes both a negative judgmental attitude and very unreal to our true selves. How do you think *you* got the idea that Christians are a bunch of stern-faced people who are against having fun in any form? Our job is *not* to pronounce judgment! God is quite able to take care of that little chore — and will someday. But until then the verdict is still out. The court isn't even in session.

Our job as Christians is to give a positive witness to the joy of being in Christ and to the great love of God for us all. The very fact that people have such a bad taste about witnessing shows both that Christians (in the past) have not put forth a positive witness and that we have allowed outsiders to *tell* us more about what constitutes "Christian actions" than we have *shown* them! There is an element of "preaching" in witness, but it should never be "preachy." There are ways that every Christian may (must) share their faith positively:

(1) The most basic way we discussed in the epistle on "living the Christian life": "Try always to live the *Golden Rule*. . ."

(2) One of the most important ways to share your faith is simply to *share your life*; who you are and what you have. Yes, witnessing by example is always absolutely necessary. It will always speak louder than words, when the actions and words are not complimentary. "Public proclamation, whether from a pulpit or in personal witnessing, is never convincing unless it is perceived as true of the life lived . . . ."[4] There is no way around it: Your witness will always be judged by the way you live your life.

You witness every time you show love, compassion, caring and acceptance! You witness every time you share your family, your home, your resources *in Christ's name*[6] with those in need of family, home, etc.

(3) But your good example is not enough. It is not complete witness in and of itself. "Yet, those who thus say: 'I need not proclaim for the way I live is my witness,' need to realize that actions are inadequate without the support of the spoken word. Deeds can only point to but never explain."[5] People will never know why you do such kindness unless you tell

them (in the right way, at the right opportunity). *It is because of what God through Christ has done for you that these things are shared.* When you don't share this (the very reason for love in our world), you cheat them of the opportunity to know Him and His love.[7] This is ultimately the most important part of witness.

It should be pretty obvious at this point that the more mature you become in Christ, the more you know about your faith, the more you strive to bring every area of your life into line with His will, the *more* effective will be your witness. I am reminded of that beautiful message found in Philippians 2:12-15:

> . . .continue to work out your salvation with fear and trembling, for it is God who works in you to will and to act according to his good purpose. Do everything without complaining or arguing, so that you may become blameless and pure, children of God without fault in a crooked and depraved generation, in which you shine like stars in the universe as you hold out the word of life . . ."

This Scripture is as true today as ever. With reverent and submissive attitudes toward God, we need to work at our faith so that He may continue to grow in us. We can never, never be part of the church if our lives are marked by petty bickering, grumbling, complaining, immature childishness.

The imagery in this New Testament passage is really breathtaking. We are like stars which shine forth in brightness against the blackness of the night. So the lives of Christians lighten the moral darkness of our world. Our very lives, by the grace of Christ, are lights holding forth the word of life. When Paul says that Christians hold forth the word of life, it is not as if we are holding out a light on a stick. The light of a star, you know, comes from within its own being. We are holding forth the example of our own very lives! We are the lights of the world *(Matthew 5:14-16)!*[8] This is sharing your faith!

STUDY/DISCUSSION QUESTIONS

1. What does the word "martyr" mean?

2. Why doesn't witnessing come easy for some Christians?

3. It is so important for every Christian to be able "to give a positive witness to the joy of being in Christ and to the great love of God." Why?

4. How do you share your faith "positively"?

5. Witness is tied to Christian maturity. How?

6. What does it mean to you to be a light to the world *(Matthew 5:14-16, Philippians 2:12-15)*?

7. Discuss why the bootblack's witness was so beautiful (footnote seven).

FOOTNOTES

[1]Almost every chapter in this series has made reference to witnessing; e.g., "Try in some way, by example or word, to share your faith in Christ Jesus daily" in Chapter 1; "As we mature, faith is being able to call people to an intelligent commitment to Christ by giving reasons for our belief" in Chapter 2; "Living the Christian life *is* a constant mental desire. . . . You should want to share it" in Chapter 3; "This kind of love naturally flows to others . . ." in Chapter 4, through Chapter 17 which says: "The real meaning of ministry for all Christians is service in the world and to one another following the example of our Master."

[2]See the chapters on: "Living the Christian Life," "Day by Day," and "Ministry and the Christian."

[3]Recently a good friend of mine, the wife of a minister, related to me an incident which caused her to have feelings of "righteous indignation." My reply to her was: "_____, I long ago stopped having feelings of righteous indignation when I realized that *I* didn't have enough *righteousness* to be *indignant* about anything!"

[4]Terry L. Miethe, *Reflections*, 1980.

[5]Ibid.

[6]There is a big difference between "humanitarian" acts of goodness *and* Christian ones. The Christian is doing the "act" because of God's love for them and their commitment to Christ. It is done *in Christ's name!* It is therefore essential, given the appropriate opportunity, that this fact also be shared with the recipient of the act of kindness. This makes it a truly complete witness.

116

[7]Ruth Graham tells this story of a simple and beautiful witness: "*The small bootblack* polished away with enthusiasm. He liked his work—turning a pair of scruffy leather shoes into a shining work of art. He liked the men who called him by name, sat in his chair, and buried their noses in the morning newspaper. He especially like the little foreign man with the funny accent.

His friendly, "Today, how you are?" let him know this man really cared how he was. What the bootblack did not know was that the man with the funny accent was from Soviet Georgia and held three earned doctoral degrees. He just kept polishing away happily.

The day came when the unhappy Ph.D. could stand it no longer. Looking down at the bootblack working so cheerfully and enthusiastically on his shoes, and thinking on his own inner misery, he put down his paper.

"Why always you so happy?" he asked.

Surprised, the bootblack paused in his polishing, sat back on his heels, scratched his head thoughtfully for a moment, then said simply, "Jesus. He loves me. He died so God could forgive my badness. He makes me happy."

The newspaper snapped up around the face of the professor and the bootblack went back to polishing his shoes.

But the brilliant professor could not escape those simple words. They were what brought him eventually to the Savior.

Years later, my husband's college major was anthropology. His beloved and admired professor was the renowned Dr. Alexander Grigolia, who found God through the simple testimony of a bootblack those many years before." Related in *By the Way* . . . in *Christianity Today*, January 1982. This illustrates the importance of a spoken witness, and that "doing" is not enough!

[8]In John 8:12, Jesus says He is the light of the world and because we follow Him we walk in the light.

19 / God and the Day's Work

A Chrstian is a steward. A Christian is a minister. A Christian is a witness. Indeed, any Christian who can justly claim that name is concerned about living for God every day of life! One of the biggest problems with the churches I know best is that the teaching and preaching seem to fail in touching the members' everyday lives. It doesn't translate in a way that the people can understand its implications in day-by-day living. Yet, the Christian lives in the world and must serve as "salt" and "light" and "leaven."[1]

The Meaning of Vocation:

The word "vocation" comes from the Latin *vocare*, "to call," and is defined as: "A summons or strong inclination to a particular state or course of action; esp: a divine call to the religious life; b: an entry into the priesthood or a religious order; 2a: The work in which a person is regularly employed: OCCUPATION . . ." Labor is important to people because it is precisely through labor that humankind receives identity and purpose in life.

Vocation means being summoned. For the Christian the one doing the calling is God. Every Christian is divinely called upon to act, to work out their priesthood *(Romans 12:1-2)*. Robert Lowry Calhoun says:

> But what is still more fundamental is that every Christian, rich or poor, ignorant or educated, Western or Eastern, has his mission in the world, his vocation that no one but he can fulfill. To find that mission and to act in line with it is vital for his personal well-being. It is vital also, as far as the life of an individual can be, for the well-being of his family, his nation, and his world.[2]

117

So vocation is essential not only for individual identity and purpose in life, but it is also vital to personal and corporate well-being. Every Christian has a calling,[3] a vocation, of God. That calling is at one and the same time universal, because all are called, and individual, in that each is called according to a person's talents and abilities.

The work of the ministry is not necessarily a special type of "religious" work as opposed to work in general.[4] All are called to be God's ministers (servants, *diakonos* means servant), to love and worship Him in everyday life, and to spread the "Good News" of His love. The

> . . . habit of picking isolated experiences and segments of human life and, for one reason or another, calling them religious can be perhaps the most insidious form of anti-religion. It denies, in effect, that religion can and should pervade all of life. If, however, religion is thought of in terms of *divine vocation*, all this falls into a different perspective. So to think is to conceive of religion as the *calling forth of a person's entire range of capacities and skills into worship and devoted work for the common good, by a power not only greater than himself but greater than the whole world in which he lives.*[5]

God's call to people bids them to "be lawyers and doctors, not less than ministers and professors. It demands the construction of homes and the rearing of children."[6]

W. R. Forrester discusses the Christian calling in clear and persuasive terms, a calling which may be "worked" regardless of one's particular job:

> Is it not the essence of the Gospel, and the message more than any other needed in our time, that we are living in a world where both persons and things have been made and are being made by a personal God with whom we can enter into personal relationships in faith and prayer? The whole Gospel, its Manger-Cradle, its Cross, its Empty Tomb, its Pentecost, is directed to make and restore personal relationships, in spite of human sin which creates barriers between man and God. And God puts meaning and purpose into our lives by His call and in our calling. If we are to be able to redeem men in our age of techniques and depersonalizing machinery, we must be able to make

real to them the great truths of Creation, Providence and Grace, as these are personalized in the doctrine of vocation. Only so can we transmit the Gospel of redemption through the media of our age to rescue souls and build up the city of God.[7]

Yes, for the Christian his/her "vocation" is being a Christian, serving Christ. Their avocation[8] is really whatever they do to earn a living: put food on the table, clothes on their backs, a roof over their heads *(Matthew 6:25-34)*. The New Testament clearly teaches that our first concern must be our *vocation* (service to God) and not our *avocation* (how we meet our physical needs).

Practical Considerations:

There are some practical considerations in regard to choosing the actual work a Christian does to make a living. But the choice is personal. We must dispel a dangerous teaching; i.e., that unless you are employed in "full-time Christian service" you are a second class citizen in God's kingdom. I have had intimate knowledge of more than one Bible college in which this message came across loud and clear in many ways. The party line was that unless you were preparing for a Christian vocation (they offered majors to train for: ordained minister, Christian education, missionary service, Christian music, and church secretary) you were somehow not as dedicated a Christian. In fact, Christians who went to universities were not only second class, but suspect.

Every job a Christian can do is holy! Every work a Christian can pursue that is not, in and of itself, contradictory to their faith can be used to serve God. I believe there are many ways of making money that would be hard for *me* to reconcile with my faith: any job where I had to use immoral tactics (lying, cheating, stealing, etc.) to "do" the work, any job where I couldn't work without in practice denying or undercutting my faith because of the demands of the job or a supervisor, etc. There are jobs which I personally consider incongruous with Christian faith; e.g., selling cigarettes, liquor, illegal drugs. Selling anything that you know will contribute to the destruction of body, mind, spirit, or personal property.[9] I believe trying to sell anything to someone who doesn't need it is immoral, or selling something you *know* is an inferior product which will not perform or last or is misrepresented.

But again, the decision of what job you choose, and whether you see it as undercutting your faith or witness, is largely a personal one. Certainly there are some jobs which tend to put one into a position of possible danger more than others. On the other hand, some jobs which are "questionable" can provide an important witness. I personally think the more you can combine a job with a life commitment in regard to investment of time and effort, the more efficient a steward you will become.

Retirement and the Christian:

O.K., so you say you had to work a job that you didn't really like, that didn't provide you with much chance to witness, minister, etc. But what about retirement? If one is talking about "service to God," a Christian can *never* retire. In this sense retirement, for the Christian, is a decidedly unchristian idea! This is the difference between retiring from a way to earn money and retiring from an eternal commitment.

Because of better public health we are having a better quality of life longer. Many who are retired are persons physically and mentally strong, with an accumulation of wisdom about life which comes from long experience. You can "retire" from a life of work to make a living into *really* productive full-time Christian service. Retired people can be the church's greatest resource! When you retire you will probably have opportunity for more complete dedication of your life to Christian service than was ever before possible. Of course, realizing this along the way, wise use of your money by way of investments, disciplined Christian study as you mature, will enable you to be far more effective in Christian service in retirement. Plan ahead for how you will use your "retirement" to serve Christ!

Dedicate each day to God! Think on how you can better serve Him tomorrow and in the years of tomorrows ahead. Try each day to do your best on the job, and do it (no matter what that job) with integrity as you strive to witness to Christ in how you do your work, how you act, and in what you say. Then "God and a day's work" will be very important and very rewarding to you and to those around you!

STUDY/DISCUSSION QUESTIONS

1. Why do you think the church is not reaching the members' everyday lives?
2. Discuss the meaning of the word "vocation."
3. Every Christian is "called" to ministry. Discuss the significance of this in your life.
4. How can you make your job more holy (used to help you better serve God)?
5. Is retirement a Christian idea?
6. Have you given some thought to how you can use your "retirement" for Christ?

FOOTNOTES

[1] *Salt* preserves and flavors. *Light* allows one to see things: examples of living, examples of God's love, etc. See Matthew 5:13-16. *Leaven* permeates and transforms. See Matthew 13:33.

[2] Robert Lowry Calhoun, *God and the Day's Work: Christian Vocation in an Unchristian World.* New York: Fleming H. Revell Company, 1943, p. vi.

[3] There have been many different opinions in the history of the church regarding the "call of God" and how one receives it. These have ranged from an almost complete mysticism (still popular in many quarters) to an almost complete rationalism. There are a host of epistemological questions and ethical problems involved in this discussion. I believe that a study of the New Testament clearly shows that all Christians are "called of God" to be ministers, servants, etc. And that all human beings are called to be Christians, if they will. Our type of service depends on our particular talents and abilities, opportunities, and the needs at a certain time *(I Corinthians 12:12 30).*

[4] See the chapter on: "Ministry and the Christian."

[5] Calhoun, *Ibid.*, p. 1.

[6] *Ibid.*, p. 2.

[7] W. R. Forrester, *Christian Vocation: Studies in Faith and Work.* being the Cunningham Lectures, 1950, in New College Edinburgh. New York: Charles Scribner's Sons, 1953, p. 21.

[8] Avocation means: "2: a subordinate occupation pursued in addition to one's vocation esp. for enjoyment: HOBBY."

[9] I am not here talking about things used for self-defense, defense of society, or national defense. We must, however, remember that defense, at least initially, is *not* aggression.

20 / The Christian and Sin

In the first discussion I said: "You have accepted Jesus as your savior. Your past sins are forgiven! Count on it." When Jesus died on the cross He bore our sins and won our freedom (*I Peter 2:24*). *Two very important comments were made in Chapter 1 regarding sin: (1) Christians do not claim to have reached any state of perfection. But they do* have the promise of God that their past sins are forgiven (*Romans 8:1*). Because our sins have been forgiven, we should not live with the burden of guilt! This sense of guilt for past sins can be devastating for a new Christian. Remember: God has wiped the slate of our past clean. This is the whole point of the gospel as it is explained by the Apostle Paul in Romans. (2) We have the promise that He will forgive our shortcomings in the future if *we are* striving to live daily for Him!

I quoted Thomas R. Kelly, in Chapter 1, that many people "follow our Lord half-way, but not the other half." The "other half" is to disown self. Kelly says there are four steps in this commitment of our "lives in unreserved obedience to Him": First is "the flaming vision . . . of an absolutely holy life." This, he says, is the "work of the Eternal One . . . ." Second, begin where you are. "Live this present moment . . . in submission and openness toward Him." The third step speaks of sin in the life of the Christian:

> If you slip and stumble and forget God for an hour, and assert your old proud self, and rely upon your own clever wisdom, don't spend too much time in anguished regrets and self-accusations but begin again, just where you are.

And fourth, Kelly says: "Don't grit your teeth and clench your fists and say, 'I will! I will!' Relax. Submit to God."[1]

Perhaps these steps will be easier if we have a better understanding of the nature of sin. What is it to "sin"? The fact of sin is so clear to biblical writers that it is scarcely argued *(Romans 1:18,3:20, I John 1:8-10)*. Basically, self-centeredness and pride are the elements found in all sin; i.e., the conviction in the final analysis, that we are the center of the universe. All sin is the attempt to live as though we were God! We deify self. It is on this basis, as I read Scripture, that I become more and more convinced the only sin recorded there is idolatry! If worshiping something else, e.g., self, others, money, power, knowledge for its own sake, we are being controlled by another "deity" and God cannot be the very center of and purpose for life!

The whole purpose of Jesus' mission to humankind was necessary because of sin. Jesus said: "I did not come to call the righteous, but sinners" *(Mark 2:17)*. Even His name spoke of His mission *(Matthew 1:21)*. John the Baptist spoke of His purpose in saying: "Behold, the Lamb of God who takes away the sin of the world" *(John 1:29)*. Preaching, from the very origin of the Church, emphasized the need for sins to be forgiven *(Acts 2:38, 5:31, 10:43)*. We are told clearly "that Christ Jesus came into the world to save sinners. . ." *(I Timothy 1:15)*.

The Greek New Testament uses a dozen or more terms for what we call, in English, sin. Here are some:

(1) *Adikia* means unrighteousness or wickedness *(Romans 1:18)*, wrongdoing, or injustice *(Romans 9:14)*. Sometimes it meant "misdeed," e.g., 2 Corinthians 12:13, Hebrews 8:12. I John 5:17 says that all *adikia* is *hamartia* (sin).

(2) *Hamartia* is used most often in the New Testament for the idea of sin. The verb equivalent to the noun means to transgress, to do wrong, to sin against God. It requires forgiving *(Mark 2:5)* and cleansing *(Hebrews 1:3)*. Paul speaks of *hamartia* almost in personal terms *(Romans 5:12,21)*. *Hamartia* has a deceptive power as is warned in Hebrews 3:13.

(3) *Anomia*—denotes lawlessness. It implies defiance of law. In Romans 6:19 *anomia* is contrasted with righteousness and holiness.

(4) *Apistia*—indicates unfaithfulness, lack of belief *(Hebrews 3:12)*, or disbelief. In Romans 3:3 it seems to mean betrayal of trust.

(5) *Asebeia*—means impiety or irreverence *(2 Timothy 2:16)* and can be translated "ungodliness."

(6) *Aselgeia*—has the idea of licentiousness, debauchery, or sensuality *(Jude 4)*. The idea is an unrestrained commitment to evil.

(7) *Echthra*—is defined as hostile feelings or actions and may best be translated "enmity" or "hostility" *(Romans 8:7)*. Paul says the work of Christ is to overcome hostility between Jew and Gentile *(Ephesians 2:14-16)*.

(8) *Kakia*—is one of the stronger terms in the New Testament for describing wickedness or depravity as opposed to virtue *(I Peter 2:16)*.

(9) *Parabasis*—makes an important contribution to the understanding of the nature of sin. It means, in part, transgression, an overstepping of the boundaries, a violation of the law. Here is a strong emphasis upon willful, or at least conscious, violation of the law *(Romans 4:15, 5:14)*. It is related to disobedience *(Hebrews 2:2)*.

(10) *Poneria*—has the meaning of wickedness, baseness, or even maliciousness. It is similar to *kikia*. Both terms are together in I Corinthians 5:8.[2]

In Scripture, the sinful condition of humankind is explained by our willful abuse of our God-given freedom. We choose the "basic course and character" of our lives (see *Genesis 3*)! Paul tells us this in a "careful and forceful analysis" in Romans 1:18-32. We could not be given the *potential* for good without also the *potential* for evil. Sin is really our choice *to be* (to exist) apart from God. It is a "natural" tendency for us to try to be independent, to live of and for ourselves. But we must not—and in Christ we cannot!

I have heard the question asked: "Was man—is man—able not to sin?" I rather like the following answer:

From the Bible, from logic, and from experience one is driven to answer, "yes and no." How high can a man jump—six feet, seven feet? Then why not eight or nine feet, or over the house? Theoretically there is no limit to the height he can jump; actually there is. In a real sense man is able not to sin. The fact that the Bible throughout holds man *guilty* for sin is conclusive for its position that man does not have to sin.[3]

The fact of the matter is this: Finally, we will all sin! We are not strong enough in our present existence, on our own ability, to truly exercise our freedom wisely without God's help.

I will close with two ideas from Scripture: (1) Let us always remember that ours is not to "judge" or "pronounce" acts of sin in others. *We* would be well disposed to use *our* energy striving to live rightly for God *(Matthew 7:3, Luke 6:41).* (2) Mark 8:34-36 reads:

If anyone wishes to come after Me, let him deny himself and take up his cross, and follow Me. For whoever wishes to save his life shall lose it; and whoever loses his life for My sake and the gospel's shall save it. For what does it profit a man to gain the whole world and forfeit his soul?

I thank God that we have chosen the way of life! Let us so live that others may see His light!

STUDY/DISCUSSION QUESTIONS

1. What does it mean to have been forgiven?
2. Why is false guilt so dangerous to the Christian?
3. How can you better live the holy life to which Thomas Kelly points us?
4. What is "sin"? What is idolatry?
5. How did Jesus' mission on earth relate to sin?
6. What do the Greek New Testament words tell you about sin?
7. How can you deal with sin in your life?

FOOTNOTES

[1]Thomas R. Kelly, *A Testament of Devotion*, p. 21-24.

[2]See Frank Stagg, *New Testament Theology*, p. 13-21.

[3]*Ibid.*

21 / The Problem of Evil

Without a doubt the most difficult problem, in its practical and theoretical implications, for the Christian to answer is the problem of evil. "Why does my loved one have to suffer so much?" "If God is so good and powerful why does He allow so much evil in the world?" You cannot be in this world very long (certainly not in the ministry long) before you hear or ask such questions! Because of the very personal, emotional nature of this problem, intellectual answers that would be considered adequate in other realms do not totally satisfy here. Yet, I believe there are good answers[1]—in fact that the Christian has the only meaningful method of dealing with evil.

This article is necessarily very limited. I strongly suggest that you think through this problem, study it, and come to some conclusions that will strengthen *your* life. Do this *before* you are forced to deal with it in the heat of emotional crisis! The problem of evil concerns the contradiction, or apparent contradiction, between the reality of evil on the one hand, and belief in the goodness and power of God on the other.

In a very general classification, the religious world has offered three main types of solution:

(1) The *monism* of some Hindu teachings, according to which the phenomenal world, with all its evil, is illusion.[2] Obviously this is not an attempt to solve the problem. It just redescribes and thus defines it away. It also leaves unexplained the evil of our suffering from the compulsive illusion of evil.

(2) The *dualism* exemplified best by ancient Zoroastrianism, with its opposed good and evil deities.[3] This

is also found in various forms in the finite deity doctrines of such modern philosophers as J. S. Mill and Edgar Brightman.

(3) Many, including John Hick, view the Christian monotheist attempt to deal with the problem as a combination of monism and dualism; i.e., ultimate *metaphysical* monism, and an *ethical* dualism.

A standard philosophical formulation of the problem of evil goes like this:

(1) If God is all-powerful, He must be able to prevent evil.

(2) If He is all-good, He must want to prevent evil.

(3) But evil exists.

(4) Therefore, God is either not all-powerful or not all-good.

The idea of "theodicy" (from the words for God and justice) is an attempt to reconcile the unlimited goodness of an all-powerful God with the reality of evil.

As you already see, the problem of evil, in its philosophical sense, gets quite involved. Actually any theory that attempts to deal with evil must address three types of evil: (1) That evil originated by human beings; i.e., moral evil or sin. (2) The physical sensations of pain caused by tornado, earthquake, etc.; i.e., natural or physical evil. And (3) the imperfection of all created things which some have called metaphysical evil.

Evil was a philosophical problem from the beginning. The problem of evil was a lifelong preoccupation of St. Augustine (born 354 A.D.—died 430) of Hippo.[4] He established the main lines of thought which were followed by the majority of Christian thinkers.[5] Before his Christian conversion, Augustine was a follower of Manichaeism.[6] It affirmed an ultimate dualism between good and evil. Good had to do with light and spirit. Evil was related to darkness and matter. Thus all physical existence was ultimately evil. Augustine rejected this dualism. He believed in a good God as the sole creator of ultimate reality. The world (material), Augustine believed, reflected the goodness of its Creator.

How did Augustine answer the questions: "What is

evil?" and "Where does it come from?" First, evil is a privation. Augustine rejected the Manichaean idea that evil was an independent reality or power. Evil is a privation, corruption, or perversion of something good. "Nothing evil exists in itself, but only as an evil aspect of some actual entity." Everything God created is good. Evil occurs *only* when beings, which are intrinsically good, become corrupted. This spoiling of God's good creation is a result of actions of free creatures, angels and men. Sin, which is their free choice, is a result of their turning away from God to a lower "good." "For when the will abandons what is above itself, and turns to what is lower, it becomes evil—not because that is evil to which it turns, but because the turning itself is wicked."[7]

Augustine held that natural evils, such as disease, were ordained by God as the consequences of the fall of mankind into sin. When man sinned, the repercussions affected the whole of physical reality. Thus all evil, either directly or indirectly, is traced to the misuse of freedom delegated to His creations by God.

There is a second main theme regarding evil in Augustine's thought. This is called the aesthetic conception of evil. Accordingly, that which sometimes appears to be evil is seen in too limited a context. It is actually a necessary element in a universe which, viewed as a total unity, is wholly good. "To thee there is no such thing as evil, and even in thy whole creation, taken as a whole, there is not."[8]

It has been said that "it is easy to make something that is not a problem a real problem in philosophy and theology and to make something that *is* a problem, basically because we are finite humans, into an *unsolvable* problem." How true! Well, then, how does a Christian deal with the very real problem of evil?

(1) I think we are driven to say that God (though He did not have to create, once He did He) had to create the best of all possible ways of obtaining the best of all possible worlds! If we have reason to believe in an all-powerful, creator, redeemer God, then this world with free human beings *must* be the best way to Ultimate Reality.

(2) Evil is inherent in the risky gift of free will! I said in the last epistle (Letter 20) that real freedom (truly being created in God's image) demands "the *potential* for good . . . also the *potential* for evil."

(3) Much of the suffering in our world can be traced directly to the evil choices people make. I have seen people marching with signs against almost everything, but never with any saying: "Down with freedom." I have, on the other hand, personally seen places with signs everywhere attesting to a freedom which did not exist (East Berlin).

(4) Scripture tells us of the reality of Satan who is free to do evil until God's final judgment. Even angels were not above "self-centeredness and pride . . . elements in all sin." Just as we sometimes try to deify self, so did Satan.

(5) Really, God has Himself entered into our pain and has become the great sufferer. In giving His Son, Christ Jesus, God allows us all to eventually be redeemed if we so choose—and without violating or lessening the reality of our free will.[9]

Thus only Christianity has a workable answer to all realms of pain and evil. The world was created and is sustained by an all-powerful and loving God. A God who was able to create us in His own image with real freedom (delegated sovereignty). Who loves us enough to suffer Himself for our redemption. And who was powerful enough to conquer evil without destroying our choice. This is why the Christian faith offers such comfort in the fact of great suffering! For the Christian there need not be any fear of the unknown or of death. In Christ, believers will know victory for eternity!

Contrary to some theological traditions which reject free will, it is not demeaning God or limiting His sovereignty to posit truly free creations. In fact, just the opposite is true. Only a God who can have the power to create free creations is really sovereign and not impotent. Only a God who can and does suffer for our evil is truly loving! Only this God is truly glorified.

God must, therefore, be all-powerful in an absolute sense and be the prime example of perfect relativity.[10] God must be immanent in and really related to the world in which we live. This is consistent with the Christian Scriptures *and* the only real answer to the problem of evil. The Gospel of John, third chapter and the sixteenth verse, reads:

> For God so loved the world, that He gave His only begotten Son, that whoever believes in him should not perish, but have eternal life.

STUDY/DISCUSSION QUESTIONS

1. Why is it so important to think through the problem of evil "*before* you are forced to deal with it in the heat of emotional crisis"?
2. How have world religions approached the problem of evil?
3. Some think the reality of evil means God is limited in power or goodness. Why?
4. Give examples of the three types of evil in your experience.
5. How did Augustine deal with the problem of evil?
6. Discuss the modern Christian's answer to evil.
7. How should a Christian deal with personal suffering?

FOOTNOTES

[1] There is a multitude of books on the problem of evil from all sides. I recommend the following: C. S. Lewis, *The Problem of Pain: The intellectual problem raised by human suffering, examined with sympathy and realism.* New York: Macmillan, 1962; Normal L. Geisler's *Philosophy of Religion.* Grand Rapids, MI: Zondervan, 1974, and *The Roots of Evil.* Zondervan, 1980; John W. Wenham, *The Goodness of God.* Downers Grove, IL: Inter Varsity Press, 1974.

[2] A confused echo of this doctrine is heard in *Christian Science*, which affirms that "evil is but an illusion, and it has no real basis. Evil is a false belief"—Mary Baker Eddy, *Science and Health*, 1934, p. 480: 23,24.

[3] A much less extreme dualism is thought to be propounded by Plato; e.g., *Timaeus* 30A and 48A.

[4]See: Terry L. Miethe, *Augustinian Bibliography, 1970-1980: With Essays on the Fundamentals of Augustinian Scholarship.* Westport, CT: Greenwood Press, 1982.

[5]The following were influenced by the Augustinian analysis: Thomas Aquinas—both of these main Augustinian themes appear in Thomas' *Summa Theologica* I, 47-49. Luther and Calvin—though not interested in developing a general theodicy, followed Augustine in his doctrine that all the evils of human life flow ultimately from the culpable fall of man. Leibniz—in his *Theodicee* (1710) employed the two Augustinian themes in his argument that this is the best of all possible worlds. C. S. Lewis—suggests that the fall of Satan had cosmic consequences, perverting the entire evolutionary process to a savage struggle for existence following Augustine *(The Problem of Pain*, p. 122-124).

[6]Manichaeism was a powerful contemporary (to Augustine) religion with Eastern and Gnostic roots. This sect was founded by the Persian prophet Mani in the end of the 3rd Century A.D.

[7]Augustine, *The City of God*, XII. 6.

[8]*Ibid., The Confessions*, VII. 13.

[9]See: Paul E. Little, *Know Why You Believe.* Downers Grove, IL: Inter Varsity Press, 1972, especially pages 80-89.

[10]See: Terry L. Miethe, *The Metaphysics of Leonard James Eslick: His Philosophy of God.* Ph.D. Dissertation at Saint Louis University, 1976. Published in limited edition by the author.

22 / Serving Christ: A Family Affair

From Eden to eternity; from the creation of the first Adam to the reign of the last Adam; from Deuteronomy 6 to Ephesians 6, God makes it clear that serving Him is a family affair. We live in a society that seems determined to reduce the importance of the home or even destroy family life altogether. Historians have long argued that the disintegration of the family unit was a major element in the decline and fall of ancient Rome. Our own society's decline in family influence is distressingly similar to that decline in the Roman Empire.[1]

Many factors could be named as having contributed to the decline in the importance of the home as a family unit: divorce, substitute parents and fatherless children, low moral standards, materialism, and strained family relations. But perhaps the most important factor in the waning importance of the home is what some call sociological detraction. This is the idea that the social functions carried on by the home have now been shifted to larger social groups. Certainly all of us who have school age children know the plight of running ourselves ragged transporting our children to and from this or that function or practice. The family has to fight for any "togetherness" time. Even the church is not guiltless. Many church activities tend to separate the family rather than unite it.

Christian education is the hope of the world! It must be the bridge over which biblical theology or biblical content is transmitted to the Christian. Christian education must answer the *why* questions (i.e., the meaning questions), not just the *how, when,* or *where* ones. There are only two divinely appointed institutions in the Bible: the home and the church.

Christian education is of the greatest importance to both of these, for neither can stand without it.

The home can and should be one of the most important parts of the teaching ministry of the church. But for this to occur we must implement the biblical theology of the home, employing our churches and our family structures for that purpose. The family unit is seen as important through what the Bible says about the home *(Genesis 2:18-24)*. The only way husband and wife can grow closer to each other is by each growing closer to God. The Bible is very clear about the parents' responsibility to instruct their children in the home in Christ. The New Testament gives no indication that we are relieved of responsibility for this instruction. God's truth must be at the center of our consciousness (our minds or reasoning ability).

The family is important because of the Bible's teaching on learning. Jesus taught by being aware, and making others aware, of feelings and attitudes. He communicated not just formal teaching, although His teaching did include that element *(Luke 11:1)*. Jesus also taught by participation. It was theory applied to the practical. The Biblical emphasis on learning in the home is quite natural. The children should be under the control of the home, more than that of any other institution. The parents bear the responsibility and have the time to set examples and establish experiences by participation. The school has the child 16 percent of the time and the home has the child 83 percent of the time (that is, if we do not give up our time in unwise aligning of priorities). Church educational programs cannot possibly do, in Christian education, what the home *must!*

We Americans have more leisure time than ever before, and yet we all wonder "where the time goes." Again it is a matter of priorities! If we would do less television watching, etc., we could better utilize the 83 percent of the time we have our children for nurture in the Lord. We should *not* let our children watch so much television! We must realize that we have a responsibility to discipline our lives for Jesus!

The family is important because of its responsibility in evangelism. Jewish children were nurtured in the Old Testament and in the faith at home! A strong case can be made for the assertion that the Jewish people survived five thousand years because of the nation's emphasis on education in the home. And a case can be made that the decay in our society is the result of a lack of strong education in the home. The New Testament examples showing household conversions indicates that evangelism through children and the family unit is natural and biblical *(Acts 16:31-34)*. We must do some rethinking in the church about our responsibilities for using the assets of our families to win other families to our Lord!

Present world conditions demand renewed emphasis on Christian education as a responsibility of the home. We are experiencing a rapid change in many cultures. Change in social structures always affects the home. Certainly now we can see the results of post-World War II materialism in our culture. It has almost destroyed us as a nation. We suffer from a permissive lack of discipline in all the social-economic and political areas of our society. It may yet destroy us!

In response, a Christian home can be and should be a powerful witness to fundamental truth and lasting values. The church can do much to strengthen the home and establish this powerful force for world evangelism. We must stop robbing the home of the time it needs to function. Ministers need to educate Christian parents to the responsibilties of discipleship and nurture in the home. We need a strong program of adult education in the church that will permeate the home and reach the world *(Matthew 28:19,20)*. Strengthened family ties will reduce the generation gap and improve the general health of society. The Bible teaches that the basic unit for Christian teaching is the family, and the family is the basic unit for building the church and civilization. Knowing and sharing the riches of God's wisdom *(Philippians 1:9-11; John 8:31,32; I Corinthians 4:1,2)* by and through the Christian family has to be the key to Biblical evangelism in the world today.

But how do we make serving Christ a family affair? Strange as it may seem, God gave us the answer to this question through Moses in Deuteronomy 6:4-9. Progress toward spiritual maturity depended, Moses obviously felt, upon the absorption and assimilation of certain truths by God's people. As new Christians, start today to apply the teaching of this Scripture in your life and in your home:

(1) Total commitment is required on the part of parents. "Hear, O Israel! The Lord is our God, the Lord is one! And

you shall love the Lord your God with all your heart and with all your soul and with all your might" *(Deuteronomy 6:4,5)*. This Scripture is quoted in Matthew 22:37; Mark 12:29,30; and Luke 10:27. The husband and wife must first have dedicated their total beings to the Lord, every aspect of their personality. We cannot accept Christ as *Savior* without accepting Him as *Lord* of our lives. It is very likely that if father and mother are not concerned about living for Christ minute by minute the rest of the family won't be, either. This is the "great commandment." Jesus, in quoting this Old Testament passage, says this is the *first* responsibility of every Christian.

"And these words, which I am commanding you today, shall be on your heart" *(Deuteronomy 6:6)*. The word, "heart," is often used in the Bible as a metaphor for the mind, the reasoning ability of a person—that which makes a human, human. Thus we have an injunction to keep this commandment of God for total commitment constantly in our minds. This presupposes a constant studying of Scripture by parents for their own growth and that of their children.

(2) Formal instruction of the children by the parents is necessary. "And you shall teach them diligently to your sons . . ." *(Deuteronomy 6:7)*. That which is to be written on the heart and taught to the children is moral and spiritual truth about God, and love for God. *Diligent* means persevering and careful in work—involving steady painstaking effort. We cannot be satisfied with reading Bible stories out of some book to our children. We *must* put aside time for formal instruction if they are to grow to be mature Christians.

(3) Informal teaching is also essential. ". . . and shall talk of them when you sit in your house and when you walk by the way and when you lie down and when you rise up" *(Deuteronomy 6:7)*. Could God have made it any more inclusive? We should, by *word* and *example*, talk of spiritual things to our children at home early in the morning, before and as we rest; when we are traveling; at all times. Speaking about Christian things should be as commonplace in our family relationships as is speaking about school, sports, or even the weather. After all, our whole lives are motivated by our love for God!

(4) If Christian parents so teach, it will result in a marked change in the character of the whole family. This is what the process of Christian maturity is all about. "And you shall bind

them as a sign on your hand and they shall be as frontals on your forehead" *(Deuteronomy 6:8)*. The truth of God and our love for God will affect what we *do* (be bound on our hands) and what we *think* and *say* (be as frontals; i.e., of, in, on, or at the front of our minds).

(5) Even our use of possessions, given to us by God in the first place, will be as if we have written God's teachings on the doorposts of our house and on our gates *(Deuteronomy 6:9)*. Not only will our lives and the lives of our children be transformed, but even our material things will be used so as to indicate that we have stamped God's will on them.

The direct result of applying God's plan for the family given by Moses will be *joint* ministry. What could be more natural to a family, or a church, that makes a total commitment to God by formal and informal instruction, than service or ministry for Christ? The most natural way in the world to serve or minister is to make your service or ministry such an integral (i.e., necessary for completeness) part of your everyday life that it becomes indistinguishable from other parts of that life. Christianity is not a way of life, it *is* life. If we are not living as Christians, we are not living, we are only existing. Thus, the Christian home must be a powerful witness to Biblical truth, a building block of a Christ-influenced society, and the key to Biblical evangelism in our time. When every member in every family in the church comes to realize that their home may and must "reflect the beauty and glow of His perfect love," serving Christ will truly be a family affair!

STUDY/DISCUSSION QUESTIONS

1. Do you think the family is declining in importance in our society? Why?

2. Why is Christian education so very important to the family?

3. How can leisure time be prioritized for Christ and His church?

4. Does television have a positive or negative effect on your family? Why?

5. How can your family be used to evangelize?

6. What does Deuteronomy 6:4-9 teach us about the importance of the home in our faith, education, and witness?

FOOTNOTES

[1]The "traditional" family (i.e., father, mother, and children) is not the only type. I consider any *person* or persons living in a dwelling a family unit. In the most real sense, every individual Christian is an important member of God's family, the Church! Consequently, through the church children's education program (even if we are single, divorced, or widowed) we have a family to help nurture.

23 / Maturing in Christ . . .

This is the last study in this series on basic aspects of faith in Christ. Much has happened in my life during the seven months since I began this book: tragedies, triumphs, and joys. Certainly the most important was that on Easter Sunday (April 11, 1982) my own son, John-Hayden, accepted Jesus as his Lord and Savior and was baptized. I long for the time when, as he matures, he will read these lessons and profit from them as I hope *you* have profited.

Though this is the end of the series, if I can be of any help to your Christian life in the future, *please* let me know how! Remember, we all have questions and need support from time to time. We must not, cannot, carry on on our own. Stay close to the church! Always have someone you can go to for help, love, and guidance. There are three last things that I want to say to you before my pen runs dry.

First, maturing in Christ will be a lifelong process of joy and personal fulfillment *if* you take your commitment seriously and work at it. The purpose of these discussions has been to help you mature! They have given more than enough information (and I hope some inspiration) with which to help you begin. They have provided Scripture references for study, listed further reading, and some very practical suggestions about living for and serving our Lord. Please use them as one of many resources to support you in your holy quest.

Though I certainly do not accept everything William James wrote, I do believe he was correct when he said: "Man alone, of all creatures of earth, can change his own pattern . . . human beings, by changing their thoughts, can change their lives." You have accepted Jesus as Savior *and* Lord. Certainly, God has had a very real part in this. Now you must continue to use your energies to both understand what that commitment really means and to share your life with others. *You must continue to change your thoughts, as you mature in Christ, if your life is to really change.* This, as we have said, will take effort, discipline, serious commitment to study Scripture and good Christian literature. You should always have a good book that you are in the process of reading!

Second, please remember, this is *very* important — if you fail in some aspect of the Christian life or make some great mistake, you *must not* feel as if God has forsaken you forever because you are no longer worthy. None of us were or are worthy. No matter what, God does not throw us on a celestial garbage heap never to love us again. You have been redeemed! God will stand by your side. God will forgive! All you have to do is sincerely ask for forgiveness. As I said in a letter to my son after his baptism:

> From now on every decision in your life should be made with your commitment to God in mind. Every day should be seen as an opportunity to *learn* more about Him and share His love with others. Yes, *every* part of your life should now begin to take on new meaning. When you do your school lessons, practice the piano, do your art, or even play you should have God in mind. "How can this help me better prepare for a life of service and love" is a question which now becomes of greatest importance to you. You have just started a life of undreamed of joys and challenges. *But a life in which you never have to worry about failure.* (emphasis added) If you are true to your commitment to God, He will be more than true to you!

Third, one final warning of importance about an attitude of legalism in the Christian life; i.e., the idea that you know it all. Recently a Baptist friend (second in command on a ministerial staff of over twelve) said to me: "When I was right out of seminary I was ready to fight about almost everything. Now I realize that most things are not that important." He was not saying that you shouldn't believe things strongly or defend them. He was saying that his attitude had changed as he matured in Christ.

None of us will ever get to the level of knowledge or perfection where we can afford to play God, to be judgmental toward others' attempts to live for Christ. Oh, to be sure, we can disagree, we can try to help others, even try to change them in a loving way. But to be "legalistic" and "negatively judgmental" toward others may reveal more about our Christian maturity than theirs! *None of us has a corner on the Truth.* As we grow in Christ, in knowledge and in commitment, so will our compassion for others and our willingness to love grow even when there are differences in belief!

And now, this is my prayer for you, from the very depths of my being, "that your love may abound still more and more in real knowledge and all discernment, so that you may approve the things that are excellent in order to be sincere and blameless until the day of Christ; having been filled with the fruit of righteousness which comes through Jesus Christ, to the glory and praise of God" *(Philippians 1:9-11).*[1]

STUDY/DISCUSSION QUESTIONS

1. Who can you go to for guidance as a Christian?
2. Are you a living part of a church?
3. What good Christian literature are you currently reading?
4. What are your short-range, intermediate, and long-range goals to help you mature in Christ? Where do you want to be in your Christian life in the next year, five years, ten, twenty, etc.?

FOOTNOTES

[1]See also: Philippians 4:4-9.

Glossary*

absolute free from imperfection, perfect—having no restriction. exception, or qualification—In Christian thought the only real, Supreme Absolute is God Himself.

aesthetics a branch of philosophy dealing with the nature of the beautiful and with judgments concerning beauty—a particular philosophical theory or conception of art or beauty.

analogy a comparison; when you reason from analogy, you conclude that, because two or more entities share one aspect they share another as well.

antithetical constituting or marked by being in direct and unequivocal opposition; syn. opposite.

apologetics traditionally denotes the reasoned defense of Christianity against intellectual objections; the attempt to establish certain elements of Christian faith as true or, at least, not demonstrably untrue—Christian apologetics is the comprehensive philosophical, theological, and factual demonstration of the truthfulness of our Christian religion.

atonement is derived basically from Anglo-Saxon—It means "a making at one," and points to a process of bringing those who are estranged into a unity. It proceeds from the love of God. In Christian thought it is the reconciliation of God and humankind through the sacrificial death of Jesus.

baptism an integral part of God's plan—that act, when one is obedient to it, by which an individual is initiated, engrafted into the body of Christ. Christians are divided on the mode of baptism—immersion, pouring, or sprinkling.

bond-servant in the New Testament, one who voluntarily puts himself in the most dedicated service under the Lordship of Christ.

born again the term referring to one who has become a Christian—see Jesus' statement in John, chapter three.

Christian evidences that discipline which examines the evidences for the validity of the historic Christian faith—usually more an internal examination; e.g., supernatural verification through fulfilled prophecy, miracles, character of Christ, the Resurrection, Christian experience, and through the character of the Bible; but some fuse apologetics and philosophy of religion with Christian evidences.

communion the Christian observance in which bread and wine, or grape juice, are partaken of as a commemoration of the death and resurrection of Christ, the Lord's Supper, etc.

covenant a formal, solemn, and binding agreement between God and humankind or an individual.

creedal having to do with a brief authoritative formula of religious belief to which all must commit.

diligent characterized by steady, earnest, and energetic application and effort.

disciple is a "learner and a doer"—one who accepts and assists in spreading the teachings of Jesus.

eternal life is the Christian teaching that the dead, and all humans alive at the time of the Second Coming of Christ, will live without end either with God or separated from Him. Most biblical references to eternal life speak of Heaven, however, and not of Hell.

exegetical to explain, interpret—in this sense an explanation or critical interpretation of a text from the Greek New Testament in English.

faith In the history of Christian thought, two tendencies concerning the concept of faith occur: (1) Faith is regarded as belief or as mental assent to some truth; e.g., about the nature of God, etc. (2) Faith is understood to be the basic orientation of the total person best described as trust, confidence, or loyalty. For our purposes: "Faith is a conscious mental desire to do the will of the God of the Bible." See: "What is Faith Really"—Letter Two.

fellowship a community of interest, activity, feeling, and experience and so much more in the Christian sense—the ongoing attempt to share God's love with each other—sharing in the most intimate ways because we are part of God's family, the church.

free will the power asserted by moral beings to choose without restraint of physical or divine necessity or causal law—It is the denial that human acts are completely determined.

grace the unmerited favor and forgiveness of God to mankind—Grace involves such other subjects as forgiveness, salvation, regeneration, repentance, and the love of God.

hypocrite   In English a hypocrite is one who deliberately and as a habit professes to be good when he is aware that he is not. —a transliteration of the Greek *hypokrites* which mostly meant play-actor—Jesus used the term of the scribes and Pharisees *(Matthew 23:27,28)* to acknowledge and condemn their actions.

immanent   remaining or operating within the domain of reality, really related to and in our sphere of experience.

immersed   the act of being plunged or dipped. Many accept this mode as the unquestionable New Testament form of baptism—the meaning of the Greek word *baptizo* transliterated "baptize" in English.

incarnation   is the "becoming flesh" of the divine Son of God in Jesus, the Christ.

inherent   involved in the constitution or essential character of something —belong by nature to a thing.

Israelites   a descendant of the Hebrew patriarch Jacob—a native or in habitant of the ancient northern kingdom of Israel—used today interchangeably with "Jews."

Judaism   a religion developed among the ancient Hebrews and characterized by belief in one God who revealed Himself to Abraham, Moses, and the Hebrew prophets and by a religious life in accordance with Scriptures and rabbinic traditions.

justification   comes from the Latin *justificatio* which was used in the Latin Vulgate to render the Greek *dikaisosis* used by Paul to signify that act by which God brings man back into proper relationship to Him God's act of remitting the sins of guilty men, and accounting them righteous, freely, by His grace, through faith in Christ.

legions   a very large number, multitude.

mammon   material wealth or possessions especially as having a debasing influence.

Mediator   title given to Jesus as He intervenes between God and humankind—Jesus is the Mediator of the new covenant *(Hebrews 9:15, 12:24)*.

ministry   the service to God and others to which every Christian is called by virtue of Christ's teaching and their commitment.

mystical   having a spiritual meaning or reality that is neither apparent to the senses nor obvious to the intelligence; based on subjective experience (as intuition or insight).

original sin in Catholic and Calvinistic tradition, the belief in the universal and hereditary sinfulness of man since the fall of Adam—It is contrasted with actual sin, which is a self-conscious violation of God's
law.

philosophy in its broadest sense the activity undertaken by those deeply
concerned with who and what they are and what everything means;
the pursuit of wisdom and truth.

pre-existence of Christ is an expression for the conviction that the life
of Jesus Christ is rooted in the being of God—It refers to the existence of the "eternal Son" or Logos which, in the fullness of time,
was made flesh.

priesthood of all believers the idea that all Christians are ministers of
Christ with duties and services to perform on the basis of a life of
commitment.

prophet one who goes forth spreading the word of God—Though an
element of foretelling (see the future) is involved in the office of
prophet, it is not nearly as prominent as some think.

Reconciler refers to Jesus' function to reconcile (to restore friendship or
harmony) between God and His creation.

reconciliation Four important New Testament passages *(Romans
5:10ff; II Corinthians 5:18ff; Ephesians 2:11ff; Colossians 1:19ff)*
treat the work of Christ in reconciliation. It means the "doing away of
an enmity, the bridging over of a quarrel." Sinners are enemies of
God. Christ died to put away our sin. Thus, Christ restores us to harmony and friendship with God.

resurrection the bodily rising of Jesus from the dead; the rising again to
life of all the human dead before the judgment—This is an essential
doctrine of Christianity *(I Corinthians 15:12-19)*.

revelation translates the Greek word *apokalypsis* and literally means "an
uncovering, a laying bare, making nakes"—the act of revealing or
communicating divine truth by God—and the disclosure of God
Himself.

righteousness acting in accord with God's will—the gift of Christ's righteousness is made by God to all who believe *(Romans 3:22)* and it is
the basis of God's verdict of justification *(Romans 5:18)*.

Sabbath In the Bible the principle is laid down that one day in seven is to
be observed as a day holy to God. In Jewish thought the Sabbath
day was the seventh day of the week observed from Friday evening
to Saturday evening as a day of rest and worship. Christians worship
on Sunday (the first day of the week) because they believe that Jesus
rose on Sunday. The Christian Sunday is not a carryover of the
Jewish Sabbath.

salvation   means the action or result of deliverance or preservation from danger or disease, implying safety, health, and prosperity—The New Testament says clearly that sin is a reality and that deliverance from it is found exclusively in Jesus Christ.

Samaritan   a native or inhabitant of Samaria which fell in 722 B.C. Like the Jews, the Samaritans suffered under the repression of the Romans. Their creed had six articles: belief in one God, in Moses the prophet, in the Law, in Mt. Gerizim as the place appointed by God for sacrifice, in the day of judgment and recompense, and in the return of Moses as Taheb, or restorer. Their belief in the resurrection is problematical.

second coming   the Christian teaching that Jesus will return in order to judge the "quick and the dead" and to establish the kingdom of God.

secular   of or relating to the wordly or temporal, not overtly or specifically religious.

selfless   the act of putting others above self in order of importance.

specialized leadership ministry   is the term sometimes used to signify individuals called to a special ministry of teaching or leading other Christians to become better ministers or servants *(Ephesians 4:11-12)*.

spiritual   of, relating to, the spirit of God in a "religious" nature.

stewardship   the individual's responsibility to manage life and property for God—"A Christian steward is someone who realizes that *everything* they have *and* all that they are, every aspect of their being, is a gift given to them by God." See: "Christian Stewardship," Letter 16.

synagogue   the house of worship and communal center of a Jewish congregation.

systematic   methodical in procedure or plan, marked by thoroughness and regularity.

tabernacle   a tent sanctuary used by the Israelites during the Exodus which happened after 430 years *(Exodus 12:40,41)* of Egyptian enslavement.

traditions   the handing down of information, beliefs, and customs by word of mouth or by example, an inherited pattern of thought or action.

transcendant   from the Latin meaning "to surpass" or "go beyond"; extending beyond the limits of all possible experience and knowledge as in Kantianism.

transformed   to be changed in character or condition—in the Christian sense, the continual process of becoming more Christ-like.

virgin birth   the term used to refer to the virgin conception of Jesus of Nazareth; i.e., the miraculous conception of Jesus by Mary without the benefit of a human father—A doctrine that is out of vogue in some theological quarters, but essential to Christian theology.

will   disposition, inclination, appetite, passion; mental powers manifested as wishing, choosing, desiring, or intending.

worship   a life of love and service expressed toward God and specific acts thereof.

Yahweh   the name of God given to the Hebrews by Him—it really consists of vowel points given to four Hebrew consonants called the Tetragrammaton—no one knows how it was originally pronounced because the Hebrews took the commandment against "using God's name in vain" so seriously that after centuries of leaving off the vowel points the pronunciation was lost.

*This glossary of terms has only basic definitions. It will in no way take the place of in-depth word studies which are necessary for a complete understanding of the words included herein. I might add: the more educated one becomes, whether informally or formally, the more one needs a dictionary! This may sound strange, like the reverse of how things should be, but it is certainly true. There are many specialty dictionaries in most every field that you will want to consult. Some examples: Van A. Harvey, A Handbook of Theological Terms, Macmillan, 1964; J. D. Douglas, The New Bible Dictionary, Eerdmans, 1965. If one gets to the place, with a very elementary knowledge of Greek, where in-depth word studies are sought then the source is: Gerhard Kittel, editor, Theological Dictionary of the New Testament, in nine volumes, Eerdmans, 1964.

Scripture Reference Index

I. OLD TESTAMENT

II. NEW TESTAMENT

II. NEW TESTAMENT (continued)

II. NEW TESTAMENT (continued)

II. NEW TESTAMENT (continued)

II. NEW TESTAMENT (continued)

One Hundred Books

This book is only the simplest of beginnings. There is a whole creation, God's creation, out there to appreciate, understand, and to share. This supplement will provide you with a much broader beginning, though still only a beginning. These books range through beginning, intermediate, and advanced levels. To some extent the level that a particular book is viewed to be on will depend on your level of development. If the material seems to be advanced, do not give up or despair. Advanced material can be mastered with serious effort and/or help. This, after all, is the challenge for one who seeks after truth and wisdom.

I make no apology that most of the books listed are quite conservative in matters of theology. After eighteen years of study at many schools and universities—public and private, conservative and liberal—I still believe the evidence supports the historic Christian position!

While most books listed represent a conservative evangelical position, I do not recommend blind acceptance of any of them. Test their claims, search out the Scriptures yourself, pray for God's guidance, as you start down the road as a seeker of truth and wisdom (John 8:32, Matthew 7:7, Luke 11:9). I know that God will continually bless you if you seek after His truth with a humble and open mind!

I. APOLOGETICS:

1. Alexander Balmain Bruce. *Apologetics; or, Christianity Defensively Stated.* Fourth Edition. New York: Charles Scribner's Sons, 1897.
2. Avery Dulles. *A History of Apologetics.* Philadelphia: Westminster Press, 1971.
3. Norman L. Geisler. *Christian Apologetics.* Grand Rapids: Baker Book House, 1976.

156

4. Michael Green. *Runaway World*. Downers Grove, IL: InterVarsity Press, 1968.
5. Clive Staples Lewis. *The Case for Christianity*. New York: Macmillan, 1956.
6. Gordon R. Lewis. *Testing Christianity's Truth Claims: Approaches to Christian Apologetics*. Chicago: Moody Press, 1976.
7. Douglas Clyde Macintosh. *The Reasonableness of Christianity*. New York: Scribner's, 1926.
8. Clark H. Pinnock. *Reason Enough: A Case for the Christian Faith*. Downers Grove: InterVarsity, 1980.
9. _____. *Set Forth Your Case: An Examination of Christianity's Credentials*. Chicago: Moody, 1971.
10. Wilbur M. Smith. *Therefore Stand: A Plea for a Vigorous Apologetic in This Critical Hour of the Christian Faith*. Natick, Mass: W. A. Widle Co., 1945.

II. THE BIBLE, GENERAL:

11. Gleason L. Archer. *Encyclopedia of Bible Difficulties*. Grand Rapids: Zondervan Publishing House, 1982.
12. Frederick Fyvie Bruce. *The Books and the Parchments: Some Chapters on the Transmission of the Bible*. Revised Edition. Westwood, N.J.: Fleming H. Revell Co., 1963.
13. Frederick W. Danker. *Multipurpose Tools for Bible Study*. Second Revised Edition. St. Louis: Concordia Publishing House, 1966.
14. James Dixon Douglas, ed. *The New Bible Dictionary*. Grand Rapids: Wm. B. Eerdmans Publishing Co., 1962.
15. Norman L. Geisler. *Decide for Yourself: How History Views the Bible*. Grand Rapids: Zondervan, 1982.
16. _____ and William E. Nix. *A General Introduction to the Bible*. Chicago: Moody, 1968.
17. Joseph Miller Gettys. *How to Enjoy Studying the Bible*. Revised Edition. Richmond: John Knox Press, 1962.
18. Henry H. Halley. *Halley's Bible Handbook: An Abbreviated Bible Commentary*. Grand Rapids: Zondervan, 1965.
19. Carl F. H. Henry, ed. *Revelation and the Bible*. Contemporary Evangelical Thought. Grand Rapids: Baker, 1958.
20. Lawrence O. Richards. *Creative Bible Study*. Grand Rapids: Zondervan, 1971.

III. THE BIBLE AND SCIENCE:

21. Gordon H. Clark. *The Philosophy of Science and Belief in God*. Nutley, N.J.: The Craig Press, 1964.
22. Robert E. D. Clark. *Darwin Before and After: An Evangelical Assessment*. Chicago: Moody, 1966.
23. Robert T. Clark and James D. Bales. *Why Scientists Accept Evolution*. Grand Rapids: Baker, 1966.

24. James H. Jauncey. *Science Returns to God*. Grand Rapids: Zondervan, 1961.
25. John W. Klotz. *Genes, Genesis, and Evolution*. St. Louis: Concordia, 1970.
26. Norman Macbeth. *Darwin Retried: An Appeal to Reason*. Boston: Gambit, 1971.
27. Henry M. Morris. *Studies in the Bible and Science*. Grand Rapids: Baker, 1966.
28. _____ and Gary E. Parker. *What is Creation Science?* San Diego: Creation-Life Publishers, Inc., 1982.
29. Evan Shute. *Flaws in the Theory of Evolution*. Nutley, N.J.: Craig, 1961.
30. A. E. Wilder Smith. *Man's Origin, Man's Destiny*. Minneapolis: Bethany House Publishers, 1975.

IV. CHRISTIAN EVIDENCES, GENERAL:

31. George P. Fisher. *Manual of Christian Evidences*. New York: Scribner's, 1899.
32. Vernon C. Grounds. *The Reason for our Hope*. Chicago: Moody, 1945.
33. Mark Hopkins. *Evidences of Christianity*. Boston: T. R. Marvin & Sons, 1909.
34. Leander S. Keyser. *A System of Christian Evidence*. Tenth Edition, Revised. Burlington, Iowa: The Lutheran Literary Board, 1950.
35. Paul E. Little. *Know Why You Believe*. Downers Grove: Inter-Varsity, 1972.
36. Josh McDowell. *Evidence That Demands a Verdict: Historical Evidences for the Christian Faith*. Arrowhead Springs, CA: Campus Crusade for Christ, Inc., 1972.
37. _____ *More Evidence That Demands a Verdict: Historical Evidences for the Christian Scriptures*. Arrowhead Springs: Campus Crusade, 1975.
38. Bernard Ramm. *Protestant Christian Evidences: A Textbook of the Truthfulness of the Christian Faith for Conservative Protestants*. Chicago: Moody, 1953.
39. C. A. Row. *A Manual of Christian Evidences*. London: Hodder and Stoughton, 1907.
40. William H. G. Thomas. *Christianity Is Christ*. London: Longmans Green and Co., 1925.

V. CHRISTIAN EVIDENCES, SPECIFIC PROBLEMS:

41. Jon A. Buell and O. Quentin Hyder. *Jesus: God, Ghost or Guru?* Grand Rapids: Zondervan, 1978.
42. F. X. Durrwell, *The Resurrection: A Biblical Study*. New York: Sheed and Ward, 1960.
43. Norman L. Geisler. *Miracles and Modern Thought*. Grand Rapids: Zondervan, 1982.

158

44. Michael Green. *I Believe in the Holy Spirit.* Grand Rapids: Eerdmans, 1975.
45. _____. *Man Alive!* Downers Grove: InterVarsity, 1967.
46. George Eldon Ladd. *I Believe in the Resurrection of Jesus.* Grand Rapids: Eerdmans, 1975.
47. C. S. Lewis. *Miracles: A Preliminary Study.* New York: Macmillan, 1947.
48. Frank Morison. *Who Moved the Stone.* London: Faber and Faber, 1930.
49. James Orr. *The Resurrection of Jesus.* Grand Rapids: Zondervan, 1965.
50. Wilbur M. Smith. *The Supernaturalness of Christ: Can We Still Believe in It?* Boston: Wilde, 1940.

VI. THE CHURCH:

51. Robert Banks. *Paul's Idea of Community: The Early House Churches in Their Historical Setting.* Grand Rapids: Eerdmans, 1980.
52. Vernard Eller. *The Outward Bound: Caravaning as the Style of the Church.* Grand Rapids: Eerdmans, 1980.
53. Edward E. Hindson. *Glory in the Church: The Coming Revival.* New York: Thomas Nelson, Inc., Publishers, 1975.
54. Fenton John Anthony Hort. *The Christian Ecclesia.* London: Macmillan, 1900.
55. Hans Küng. *The Church.* New York: Sheed and Ward, 1967.
56. David Martyn Lloyd-Jones. *The Basis of Christian Unity.* Grand Rapids: Eerdmans, 1963.
57. William Robinson. *The Biblical Doctrine of the Church.* Revised Edition. St. Louis, MO: The Bethany Press, 1960.
58. David Elton Trueblood. *The Company of the Committed.* New York: Harper & Row Publishers, 1961.
59. _____. *The Incendiary Fellowship.* New York: Harper & Row, 1967.
60. Ray Stedman. *Body Life: The Church Comes Alive.* Glendale, CA: Regal Books, 1972.

VII. THE NEW TESTAMENT:

61. Glenn W. Barker, William L. Lane, and J. Ramsey Michaels. *The New Testament Speaks.* New York: Harper & Row, 1969.
62. F. F. Bruce. *The Defense of the Gospel in the New Testament.* Grand Rapids: Eerdmans, 1977.
63. _____. *New Testament Development of Old Testament Themes.* Grand Rapids: Eerdmans, 1968.
64. _____. *The New Testament Documents: Are They Reliable?* Grand Rapids: Eerdmans, 1953.
65. _____. *The Message of the New Testament.* Grand Rapids: Eerdmans, 1972.

66. Charles Rosenbury Erdman. *Commentaries on the New Testament Books.* 17 Volumes. Philadelphia: Westminster, 1916–36.
67. Donald Guthrie. *New Testament Introduction.* Downers Grove: InterVarsity, 1971.
68. Everett Falconer Harrison. *Introduction to the New Testament.* Second Edition. Grand Rapids: Eerdmans, 1971.
69. Frank Stagg. *New Testament Theology.* Nashville: Broadman Press, 1962.
70. Merrill Frederick Unger. *Archaeology and the New Testament.* Grand Rapids: Zondervan, 1962.

VIII. THE OLD TESTAMENT:

71. Oswald T. Allis. *The Old Testament: Its Claims and Its Critics.* Nutley, N.J.: Presbyterian and Reformed Publishing Company, 1972.
72. Gleason L. Archer, Jr. *A Survey of Old Testament Introduction.* Chicago: Moody, 1964.
73. F. F. Bruce. *The Christian Approach to the Old Testament.* London: InterVarsity, 1955.
74. R. K. Harrison. *Introduction to the Old Testament.* Grand Rapids: Eerdmans, 1969.
75. C. F. Keil and F. Delitzsch. *Biblical Commentary on the Old Testament.* 25 Volumes. Grand Rapids: Eerdmans reprint. Originally published in 1875.
76. K. A. Kitchen. *Ancient Orient and Old Testament.* Downers Grove: InterVarsity, 1966.
77. James Orr. *The Problem of the Old Testament.* New York: Scribner's, 1931.
78. Samuel J. Schultz. *Old Testament Speaks.* New York: Harper and Brothers, 1960.
79. Edward Joseph Young. *An Introduction to the Old Testament.* Revised Edition. Grand Rapids: Eerdmans, 1960.
80. Merrill F. Unger. *Archaeology and the Old Testament.* Grand Rapids: Zondervan, 1966.

IX. PHILOSOPHY OF RELIGION:

81. Colin Brown. *Philosophy and the Christian Faith: A Historical Sketch from the Middle Ages to the Present Day.* Downers Grove: InterVarsity, 1969.
82. Norman L. Geisler, ed. *Biblical Errancy: An Analysis of its Philosophical Roots.* Grand Rapids: Zondervan, 1981.
83. _____. Philosophy of Religion. Grand Rapids: Zondervan, 1974.
84. _____ and Paul Feinberg. *Introduction to Philosophy: A Christian Perspective.* Grand Rapids: Baker, 1979.
85. Stuart C. Hackett. *The Resurrection of Theism: Prolegomena to Christian Apology.* Grand Rapids: Baker, 1982.

86. James Orr. *The Christian View of God and the World.* Edinburgh: Andrew Elliot, 1902.
87. Richard L. Purtill. *Reason to Believe.* Grand Rapids: Eerdmans, 1974.
88. Samuel M. Thompson. *A Modern Philosophy of Religion.* Chicago: Henry Regnery Company, 1955.
89. D. Elton Trueblood. *Philosophy of Religion.* New York: Harper and Row, 1957.
90. Warren C. Young. *A Christian Approach to Philosophy.* Grand Rapids: Baker, 1954.

X. THEOLOGY:

91. Alexander Campbell. *The Christian System: In Reference to the Union of Christians, and a Restoration of Primitive Christianity, as Plead in the Current Reformation.* Nashville: Gospel Advocate Company, 1956.
92. Charles G. Finney. *Finney's Systematic Theology.* Minneapolis: Bethany House Publishers, 1976.
93. R. T. France. *The Living God.* Downers Grove: InterVarsity, 1970.
94. Carl F. H. Henry. *God, Revelation and Authority.* 5 Volumes. Waco, Texas: Word Books, Publisher, 1976-83.
95. _____. *Frontiers in Modern Theology: A Critique of Current Theological Trends.* Chicago: Moody, 1965.
96. H. R. Mackintosh. *The Doctrine of the Person of Jesus Christ.* New York: Scribner's, 1931.
97. Robert Milligan. *Exposition and Defense of the Scheme of Redemption: As it is Revealed and Taught in the Holy Scriptures.* Nashville: Gospel Advocate, 1869.
98. Clark H. Pinnock, ed. *Grace Unlimited.* Minneapolis: Bethany House Publishers, 1975.
99. _____ and David F. Wells. *Toward a Theology for the Future.* Carol Stream, IL: Creation House, 1971.
100. John R. W. Stott. *Basic Christianity.* Downers Grove: InterVarsity, 1971.